BASS
MYTHS
EXPLODED

BASS MYTHS EXPLODED

Newest Ways to Catch Largemouths

JERRY GIBBS

Photos by the Author
Drawings by Paul Geisert

David McKay Company, Inc.

New York

Library of Congress Cataloging in Publication Data
Gibbs, Jerry.
Bass myths exploded.

Includes index.
1. Largemouth bass fishing.   2. Largemouth
bass—Behavior. I. Title.
SH681.G5   799.1′7′58   78-2819
ISBN 0-679-50859-7

10 9 8 7 6 5 4 3 2 1

Manufactured in the United States of America
Designed by Remo R. Duchi

For Judy,
who kept a light burning

Foreword

It was the kind of midsummer day when the sun bounced back off the water in a searing flash, and even the cicadas sounded drowsy. Nothing was moving, of course, and fishing was terrible. Suddenly, a bulging shadow pushing a good-sized v-wake appeared behind the spinner bait I was buzzing across the surface. The wake came on, Jaws-like, *dum, dum, dum.* I tightened inside, slowed my retrieve. Instantly the wake was gone. After beating the spot to a froth with more fruitless casts, I turned to my companion, Grits Gresham, the outdoor writer and outdoor tv show personality.

"What do you do when you see a bass behind your bait? Keep it moving the same speed, slow it down, or speed it up?"

"It doesn't make any difference," he said.

"How come?"

"Because whatever you do will be wrong!"

He's right, of course. Bass fishermen get accustomed to taking beatings from their favorite fish. The big ones really do get away. You really should have been here yesterday. It looks as though this will be the latest spring in history. Rain is predicted for Saturday. You won't have a chartreuse Big-O when that's all they're hitting. I could go on and on listing the headaches.

We get that way because living through these experiences and shrugging them off are the only true dues you have to pay to join the great fraternity of North American bass fishermen. Like Santiago, Hemingway's hero of *The Old Man and the Sea,* you will not remember when you attained humility, but attain it you will.

For all his marvelous qualities of availability and fighting spirit, the bass can be frustratingly difficult to catch on anything like a regular basis. When you spend empty hours making hundreds of casts and patrolling acres of water, you wonder, "Where the devil are they? What in God's name are they doing? What do they want?"

You remember and cherish the days you get the answers to those questions.

If I could be granted the mythical anything-you-want wish, other than the obvious desires for long life, good health, and a pile of money, I would opt for a strange request. Just once, I'd like to walk over the top of a transparent bass lake with all its life revealed to my eyes. In my fantasy, I say, "Aw hah! There the buggers are, in thirty feet of water off that point, or suspended in the shadows of drowned timber, or moving off in feeding lanes to scatter in the bushes. Now I know your secrets, and you will bedevil me no more."

Jerry Gibbs not only shares my fantasy, he has tried to make it happen. Scuba diving in bassy places has brought him eyeball to eyeball with the fish we love best, and he has indeed learned some of their secrets.

The secrets he has learned—plus hundreds of other experiences, observations, and theories—make this a terrific book.

Why another bass book? I asked myself the same question. There are a lot around, and I can tell you that the world would be better off if many of them were still trees. But Jerry has brought to this book the same credentials that made him Fishing Editor of *Outdoor Life*—an inquiring mind, tremendous field experience, and an engaging writing style. This book will not make your bass lakes transparent, but it will come as close as possible. By sharing the experiences and observations of Jerry and his friends, you will open up your thinking so that when you look at a patch of water your mind will be down there with the fish. Indeed, what *are* they doing?

The boys on the play-for-pay bass tournament circuit have a way of labeling one another as either good "fish finders" or good "fish catchers." It has always seemed to me that the fish finders should have a big edge. After all, if we can't locate fish, our fish-catching skills won't help.

So here you go then into the best thing I've seen yet on the routines, mysteries, and secrets of the bass' world. There is knowledge here that you can translate into more than angling success. It will broaden your days on the water the way the sight of the cardinal did, and the whistle of the bobwhites. Knowing more, you will feel more.

The great angling editors of big-time outdoor magazines have a record of producing strong books. One doesn't get into the ring with McClane, Bergman, Brooks, Lucas, Trueblood, Circle, and Co. with half-baked ideas and shoddy writing. Jerry need not worry. He has come out smokin', and you will be the winner in this sparkling, information-packed look into why bass do the crazy things they do and what we can do about it to catch 'em.

LAMAR UNDERWOOD
Editor
Outdoor Life

Contents

Foreword: *Lamar Underwood*   vii
Acknowledgments   xiii

Author's Preface   xv

The Beginning   1

1   Where Are the Bass?   5
     Wind and Currents · Clear Water · Roaming
     Bass · Schooling Bass · Bass in Supercover ·
     Tactics

2   How Weather Affects Bass   41
     Seasons · Weather Trends · Storms · Wind ·
     Hot-Weather · Cold-Weather Environment

3   How Light and Color Affect Bass   67
     How Bass See · When Vision Counts Less ·
     Night Fishing · Moon Phases · Color Preference ·
     How Color Reacts · Lures · Line

4   Sounds That Turn Bass Off and On   95
     Bass and Boat Noise · Sounds and Lures

5   How Bass Strike Lures   115
        Plastic Lures · Plugs · Spinnerbaits · Shiner
        Minnows · Environmental Conditions · Physical
        Condition · Bass Size and Seasons ·
        Individualism · Positive and Negative Responses ·
        Tackle

6   New Lines on the Natural History of Largemouth Bass 149
        Spawn Factors · Courting Behavior · Spawning
        and Guarding Bass · Post-Spawn · Growth ·
        Bass Biology Vital to Fishing · Curious Bass
        Behavior and Theories to Ponder

7   Bass and Man   175
        How to Enter the Bass World · How Angling
        Affects Bass · Releasing Fish · Hands-Off
        Policies No Longer Work · Hybrids

8   Reflections on Bass Watching   193

     Index   197

Acknowledgments

There are too many individuals who helped this book come into being to list separately. Instead, I am going to have to collect a great many fierce individualists into groups based more or less on job description (they'll love that). If you helped, you know, so thanks to . . .

Countless fishermen with whom I've shared a boat or mud bottom in foul weather and fair across the nation.

The biologists, behaviorists, and other kinds of scientists whom I've argued with endlessly and kept up half the night.

The photographers, film makers, and artists who were seeing things I wasn't but, taught me how.

The divers who kept me company watching fish or minding my bubbles when they'd rather have been digging for artifacts or chasing mermaids.

The builders of fine fishing tackle, whose ability to create equipment that works comes from deep knowledge and insight into fish behavior—and who were happy to share that with me.

Editors who let me journey to the right places at the right time so the work could be done.

The cantankerous, coy, and always fascinating fish that all this work is about.

Chet Fish, who is the editor and also responsible for getting the entire project going in the first place.

Author's Preface

The seed for this book was planted back in 1953, although I didn't know it then. That's twenty-five years ago, and that was when I launched my diving career, combing the Eastern seaboard to obtain the needed equipment, which was just coming in from France and later Italy. I've been lucky enough to explore the underwater world over much of the country—including Atlantic and Pacific Oceans—plus the Caribbean and Mediterranean.

Over the years there has been a battle over which would claim most of my time, diving or sport fishing. Then in 1972, when I went to work as the fishing editor of *Outdoor Life* magazine, I became able to devote full time to studying fish both above and below water. Of the thousands of miles I traveled each year many of them have been in quest of the largemouth bass. The diving and angling research for this book have taken place across the nation— in the desert lakes of the Southwest, the frigid waters of southern Quebec at the northern extremity of the largemouth's range, in dingy farm ponds in the Midwest, in coastal rivers, the quarries of the East, and the crystal-clear springs of Florida.

Though I have kept no record of underwater hours logged, specifically aimed at producing this work, I remember days that were almost entirely spent in the water until the skin around my fingertips withered and finally began to peel.

It was during this period that I met Glen Lau, a film producer, the creator of the documentary *Bigmouth,* which followed the cycle of the largemouth bass from birth to death. Glen generously shared many of his findings and diving experiences with me, cluing me to look for particular phenomena it had taken him years to discover and which would have certainly taken me just as long.

The ever-questing mind of Paul Johnson, director of research and development for the Berkley Company, was responsible for launching a study of bass vision. That study lead me to meet Donald F. McCoy, behavioral scientist at the University of Kentucky. Dr. McCoy's experiments on largemouths had been underway for some years.

The work of these people helped me better focus on the research I had already done and had yet to do.

Hundreds of hours of personal abovewater and underwater work went into the making of this volume, and that's not counting the years of research done by the aforementioned and other professionals whose expertise helped concentrate my own research.

For all of that, tomorrow we will certainly discover something new about largemouth bass, the most popular gamefish in the United States.

J.G.

BASS
MYTHS
EXPLODED

The Beginning

My favorite kind of bass fishing may not be exactly like yours, but in the end that doesn't really matter. We're still involved with the same fish, you and I. The scientific community calls him *Micropterus salmoides*. Fishermen call him largemouth bass. Or bigmouth, hawgbelly, lunker, kegjaw, and a lot of other things sometimes.

Maybe you hunt this fish in fast boats in the big reservoirs or perhaps at a more subdued pace in smaller shady natural lakes. Maybe you like your bassing in the little pothole-size ponds with fish in them so big you still get shaky thinking about them right now. The kind of country where I started becoming serious about this sport shaped the things that mean bass fishing to me.

I started a long time ago, it seems, in and around the Currituck Sound country, North Carolina, when you had two choices of tackle: (1) a flyrod outfit, or (2) an old knuckle-duster bait-casting rig with braided line on it. That early fishing was in shallow water in creeks, ponds, or the big Sound itself. Something still starts going in me when I catch the special fragrance of tidal mud mixed with brackish water.

I like the way the wind hurries cloud shadows over the marsh grasses no matter what place it is. I'll always be a sucker for some backwoods pond with the morning sun working shafts of light through sentinel stands of cypress or pines, depending on whether my pond is in the North or South. I like big basso-voice bullfrogs baying madly in the moonlight. I cherish the chance to see eagles or hawks spiraling high and free while I sit the afternoon heat away in a battered skiff, suffering the buzzing mockery of redwinged blackbirds in the bulrushes. At first light and at dusk, I look for a deer to float suddenly out of forest gloom, and for the ribbons of blue wood smoke that catch in dead tree limbs before the wind takes them all away.

The real reason that I'm there, of course, is to work an odd-looking bit of wood or plastic, or hair, cork, and feather, along the edge of whatever kind of plant is growing where I happen to be at the moment. You know the way it happens. Sometimes you'll see him coming, pushing dead husks out of the way, and other times there'll be no warning at all. He'll crush your top-water bait in one awesome, explosive attack, turn sharp, and when, in the next moment, he realizes there is nowhere deep to go, he'll come up. Maybe it will be only that once, maybe more. But you'll have that first image painted against the low-slung bank, his mouth agape, gill covers spread, rakers blood red, the white-bellied dark-backed length and breadth of him shaking with violence in the soft light. You will forget about the deer, the hawks, the frogs, and the wood smoke, and for however long it lasts you'll be lost in primitive combat that skill and a little luck will help you win.

However it ends, you'll have some time afterward to get your breathing back to normal and maybe crack the stopper on an ancient thermos filled with lukewarm coffee.

I like it other ways, too, but that's the way I like it best. This kind of thing becomes habit-forming, doesn't it? Somehow there is never enough. And what about the belligerent creature without which we would have none of it? Probably just like you, I wanted to know more and more about this wide-mouthed predator we seek in so many different places across the continent. I learned a lot from other fishermen like you, young ones and old-timers. Some of the things made sense and helped me make catches when the odds were against it. Some other things I heard were hard to buy. It was only natural to continue searching for the answers by fishing.

There came a time, though, when I wanted to learn in a different way, to see more than I could in a boat or on a bank. It was time to enter the bass's world myself. I wasn't the first. Pioneer angler-divers not long before me had begun gleaning information about the largemouth that has added to our total knowledge of the species. My contribution, I hoped, would clear up some beliefs that seemed to border on superstition—pass-along tales whose suspected truths were never consistent.

I had been an avid sport diver as a youth. Now it was time to retune those skills and work unused muscles back into shape. A lot had happened to the world of free diving since I'd bowed out. I found myself enrolled in courses, reading seemingly endless texts, and buying more equipment than I believed was actually needed.

It came together finally. The day, some years ago, when the water's surface closed overhead and I re-entered the fish's world, was the beginning of an ongoing adventure. It was also the beginning of the end of a lot of myths that revolved around bass and bass fishing. A lot of time and work have gone into the project. The underwater world does not relinquish the secrets of its inhabitants easily.

Was it worthwhile? I believe that when you've finished these pages you will have not only new insights about the largemouth that will make you a better angler, but also a new respect for the species. If I've accomplished that, then yes, it was worthwhile. All of it.

1

Where Are The Bass?

Despite the vast quantity of information that has been forthcoming on the largemouth bass during the past several years, many fishermen are still confused. They have a right to be. One trouble is that too much of the data on the behavior of largemouths is served up in sweeping statements. We learn that bass do this or do not do that, as though each fish were cast from one mold and wired according to one schematic diagram. We even receive conflicting reports from researchers who have tracked bass through telemetry—that method in which a miniature signal-emitting transmitter is implanted into the fish.

What, for example, is a fisherman to believe when one authoritative source maintains that a hooked and released bass will not take a lure again for many days, while another expert on bass insists that a hooked and released laregmouth can be coaxed to hit a lure again very soon—the next day, or even the day on which he was first caught?

What usually happens is that if an angler discovers on his next fishing trip that some supposed truth proves completely erroneous, he summarily discards the item. In truth, the piece of information may be quite accurate under certain conditions. How come? Bass populations, like other animal populations, are made up of individuals. What we are faced with is *many* types of bass behavior. There is absolutely no substitute for learning how bass react in the specific lake or river that you will regularly fish. Even after you have established patterns of behavior, the fish will occasionally throw you a curve. There's that matter of individuality again.

Good bass fishermen learn to take advantage of bass-behavior generalities but are flexible enough to alter their tactics when standard approaches fail to produce fish. The fisherman's big danger is that he will become locked in on the idea that certain bass behavior is true no matter what. Many of the old myths about largemouths have fallen into disfavor, but you'd be surprised how many of the currently accepted "truths" about bass are frequently not really true at all. The matter of location is an excellent example.

Most successful fishermen know that the primary key to bass location is cover. Next in importance is the proximity of prey. In various circumstances, the pH, oxygen, temperature, and water clarity (light) vie in importance for determining the whereabouts of bigmouths. Cover has always seemed to be the main item. How many times have you heard it said, "Find cover and you've found bass"? It's not true.

As you know, cover of an infinite variety is used by bass that are holding to one spot to rest or are hiding in ambush. But even then, the fish may be some distance from it. Cover is not necessarily used by roaming bass, and roaming bass are quite likely to smash your lures ferociously. Someday science may discover precise reasons for off-cover location, but from a practical fisherman's standpoint, I can assure you from my own observations that bass sometimes do position themselves 70 to 140 feet or more from heavy cover. What are some of the situations in which they behave this way?

Wind And Currents

Summer and fall are two of the key periods for bass to locate some distance from the security of cover. This is a definite stationing behavior, not a free-roaming activity. I believe wind greatly influences this positioning, though some observers have reported seeing no change in bass behavior during windy weather. Contradictory? Of course. This is but one example of individuality among various bass populations. Apparent contradictions will continually crop up as we go along.

Essentially what I've found is that many bass groups head into

In some kinds of cover, a vertical presentation is preferred. Though bass could be taken by casting and retrieving in the normal way, a tiny lure or small jig flipped by flyrod and allowed to sink parallel to old pilings is often the more successful method. Here author has flipped a tiny metal flyrod spoon to piling and is preparing to use wrist flex to bring lure up vertically.

wind. So there was some basis for the old belief that you should fish a shore onto which wind is blowing. But what you should fish is not the actual shore or cover. What happens is that small aquatic organisms are moved by wind-driven currents. Baitfish follow prey drifting on these currents. If the wind-driven current is strong enough, the baitfish themselves may be moved.

It appears as though the bass, in their eagerness to devour moving forage, head in the direction from which this forage is coming. Salt-water anglers know the effectiveness of spreading a chum slick that will bring predatory species from some distance to the source of the food. The situation with bass is not much different. Largemouths suspend (hold between surface and bottom at a point that allows them to intercept food) as they feed and move away from cover toward the moving food source. The way to productively fish for these bass with artificial lures is to move out from the shore cover and then bring your lures back in the direction the wind is blowing. If you bring your lures quartering on an angle from the wind direction, you'll catch fewer fish. If you retrieve your lures 90 degrees from the direction of the wind or into the wind, you will probably be unsuccessful.

I've seen bass move from shore cover into the currents. And I find that fish that have been using such cover as offshore reefs, shoals, underwater islands, or points that extend far from shore are even more inclined to move away from their security than are the near-shore fish. The reason is probably that these offshore bass have the safety of deeper water immediately around them.

Clear Water

How many times have you gone fishless while working prime target areas such as weedlines, dropoffs, a line of rock rubble, a path of weed clumps, timber, or a ridge, along which you knew bass simply had to move or hold? You probably worked one such area, then another and another, trying to find the bass. Experience in many other lakes proved the validity of fishing such places. You've caught fish close to similar cover uncountable times. What makes these places productive in one area and not in another?

I'm still convinced that bass generally like to relate to some object as they move. Yet time after time from an underwater vantage point, I've observed them holding or moving quite some distance from any bottom irregularities. Then something dawned on me. In such situations, I was usually able to see the fuzzy outline of some sort of interesting structure at the limits of my underwater vision. Couldn't the bass see it? They must. Piecing the evidence together, I came up with a conclusion: as the water clarity increased, fish movements frequently occurred farther from cover or bottom irregularities. Evidently as long as bass can discern some shape that indicates safety or gives them their bearings, they are content to ease away from the kinds of places where we like to cast our lures. Usually I found that bass moved toward deeper water when they left cover. But sometimes I found them in what most fishermen would describe as barren areas fairly near the shore. Why? Ultimately I believe it was because such areas were in shade. Therefore, you might argue that such shade does in effect become a kind of cover.

All well and good, but are such off-cover fish inclined to take a lure or bait? It's true that in such locations the bass may be in a nonfeeding attitude. But when they are ready to feed, yes they will do so right there if something becomes available. These fish do not immediately move into ambush position in the thick of cover, as is so often believed. They may do so after a while on some occasions, but they also feed quite actively off-cover when they are ready and when food is available. Let's look further at this off-cover behavior.

I do not know if bass can see objects in clear water as far away as humans can. Indeed some researchers believe the fish are relatively nearsighted. Others disagree. But few will argue that bass lack the ability to detect distant moving objects through some kind of sensory perception. Might bass not just as well be able to detect stationary structures from which they can recognize different territories?

Perhaps, just as humans do, bass may also develop a sense of direction simply through familiarity with a territory. Though they may move even completely out of sight of cover, they are surely quite aware in which direction it lies.

I eventually proved this hunch to my satisfaction by beginning to catch bass off-cover in low-visibility conditions. I do not believe the bass could see even a faint outline of the cover under such conditions. Upon subsequent investigation I certainly could not. Does this finding refute the clear-water theory—bass holding just at the edge of visibility of cover? Certainly not. It just means bass are using means other than sight to keep track of the direction in which cover lies. Low visibility itself may be a form of cover, lending a feeling of safety to the bass. To you as an angler, then, it will pay to fish a good distance from as well as around what appears to be the appropriate bass cover, where tradition says you ought to be tossing your lures.

Roaming Bass

For fifteen minutes I had been kneeling in my diving outfit in a little gully in 18 feet of clear water, watching four huge largemouth bass. They were tight against a nearly impossible-to-fish tangle of tree branches. The seeming smugness with which they held suspended there was infuriating.

Suddenly I caught a movement off to the left. A loose school of five slightly smaller fish was moving toward me. They traveled at a leisurely pace and passed behind me, so I pivoted to watch. As they eased away beyond the blue-green vanishing point of the beautiful Florida spring, I idly wondered where they might be going and why. It was not until I had viewed such traveling groups several more times that I began to realize that here indeed was another form of bass behavior.

Since then I have seen and followed may groups of fish that were moving steadily along without haste. Some of these bass swam out from shore though following the contours of the shoreline. Others moved quite some distance from shore out into open water. These offshore fish had no cover in which to hide. Even the bass that swam nearer the shoreline seemed unconcerned with keeping cover relatively close at hand. The fish I observed swam in depths varying from about 8 to 20 feet. Why did they do it?

I believe there were two reasons: (1) to establish new holding territory, and (2) to locate schools of forage fish. It had been popularly thought that bass consistently maintain deeper-water holding stations and then move into the shallows at various times in order to feed. Largemouths actually establish many home areas during the course of a year. Many of these are in shallow water, though deeper water is nearby. Water conditions and the movements of prey dictate these holding places. Biologists Robert Warden Jr. of Forestry, Fisheries and Wildlife Development for the T.V.A., Muscle Shoals, Alabama, and Wendell Lorio of Mississippi State University, using tiny transmitters implanted into the bodies of bass, found that the fish they were studying established several home areas and maintained each for several days to two weeks or more. These researchers also found that when the fish moved to new holding locations, they did so over deep water.

Why am I convinced that the other reason for open-water roaming is to locate forage-fish populations? Time after time I've located groups of open-water fish suspended, not moving, below schools of bait—generally shad.

How can you fish the migrating bass groups? The only practical way is by trolling. The moving fish show no signs of fear from boats that make trolling passes near them. Intercepting roaming fish by casting would be more difficult, though I suspect that if you concentrate your fishing on one lake you will learn certain key places past which the fish will swim at fairly predictable periods. Narrows and saddles between islands are likely spots. When open-water fish suspended beneath schools of forage decide to feed, it is usually no problem to locate them and enjoy fast sport. This is an off-cover situation that can be enjoyed to the fullest by keeping some specialized tricks in mind.

Schooling Bass

Perhaps you have experienced the frantic sport that occurs when largemouths tear into schools of threadfin shad. If not, you owe it to yourself to visit one of the Southern or Western lakes where such behavior occurs.

Though the wild schooling periods are relatively brief, this type of activity is often sought by anglers for its sheer excitement. Forage fish churn the surface or leap entirely free. You are often able to connect with bass at one location, only to have them sound and then reappear father away. If you run with the schools, you may get into action several times before the lake reverts to dead calm. By looking around, you may not be able to discern any reason for the surface action occurring at the particular spot. No cover in the form of trees, islands, or fence lines protrudes through the surface slick. Why did the bass choose this place to attack?

Chances are that the bait school was forced to close ranks there in a sudden movement. Both this quick motion and the fact that by closing together the shad became even easier pickings probably triggered the largemouths. If you search the area with a depth finder you will probably find that the bottom rises in a hump in this location. Either that or there will be a surrounding bottom contour tightening where underwater islands squeeze close and form a kind of pass through which the schools of bait must run.

Anglers who are aware of such underwater configurations find that they can expect explosive action day after day for many weeks in the same spot at approximately the same time

There is another kind of place where surface schooling action occurs away from cover, and here there is no subsurface structure to compress the bait schools. Shad usually move along a given route farther and farther offshore with the bass hovering below. Finally, for reasons of their own, the baitfish check their headway and mill in great masses. At this point the bass—which have been following but not harassing the shad since the forage passed the last compacting point—will frequently tear into the school again. On large reservoirs this action can occur miles from shore. Anglers not aware of it usually stumble upon the melee while under way to another spot. Careful study, however, can result in your being able to tap this action regularly. During these schooling periods, most bright, flashy lures or bucktail jigs of the appropriate size will take the fish.

Bass in Supercover

Awareness of all the preceding behavior patterns will help you locate bass in off-cover situations. In contrast, largemouths may be right in the kind of cover you suspect though you can't "find" them with your lures. Of course it will be the bass that do the locating if you're able to make the proper presentation of lure or natural bait. Therein lies a larger problem than you might expect.

When I first began to visually dismantle bass cover underwater, I was horrified. Oh, there were some situations that I had expected, and which would not be terribly difficult for a fisherman to work abovewater from a boat or by casting along shore. But the others! I was left with shaken faith that my lures were ever correctly presented. It must be sheer chance that bass ever take a lure, I thought.

Root network of grasses, which extend through surface and appear as solid islands of grass, make ideal cover for largemouths. The only way to work this kind of situation is to crawl weedless lures over solid matts toward your boat, letting the baits fall into holes as they will. The last chance is at the border of cover. Here, let the lure drop.

Then I found myself wondering what kind of success fishermen would have if we could properly present lures to bass all the time instead of having to rely on coaxing them to charge from their dens—for that is all we do most of the time. If we could ever get consistency in presentation under extreme conditions, I believe our catch scores would soar. Still, after seeing complex underwater bass jungles close up, I'd be happier if the odds were a little more in our favor. We are facing some tough problems.

First you must cease to believe that above-surface shoreline consistently gives you an extremely accurate reading of what exists below. Sometimes it does. But there are more times than I care to remember when it does not.

Steep cliffs with near-vertical walls seem to be the most accurate indications of what exists underwater. Even these can be deceiving. Experience tells you that normally the vertical walls continue right down underwater, and usually they do, with some little ledging jutting from them. But I've encountered situations where a minor underwater ledge breaks into a lovely rocky peninsula extending quite far from the shoreline. This peninsula or underwater point can hold fish itself, and often such structures have still further branching and other irregularities that hold fish. If weather conditions are such that you would not normally be fishing the steep walls (late spring and summer typically), you might very easily pass such an area. Just reading the abovewater shoreline would fail to show you what was below.

Timber is another example of how an abovewater perspective can be misleading. Areas with scattered standing timber can usually be doped out pretty quickly. But what about lakes where whole forests of dead standing timber remain? Take a lake like Toledo Bend, for example. Located on the Texas-Louisiana border, this lake is literally a maze of the bones of former forests.

To the newcomer everything looks the same. Go out on a misty morning while the jagged gray trees reach up and out among moving tendrils of fog. You may easily become lost. Veterans have learned to handle such situations. It is not just the timber that holds the fish, but bottom contours in the form of ridges and humps as well. In fact, some stands of timber that look just like others nearby may be tremendously productive simply because of what they are fastened to down below. or because of the kind of bottom contour lying near them.

Without thorough investigation on your part, all the short docks that poke out from summer houses may appear the same. If you

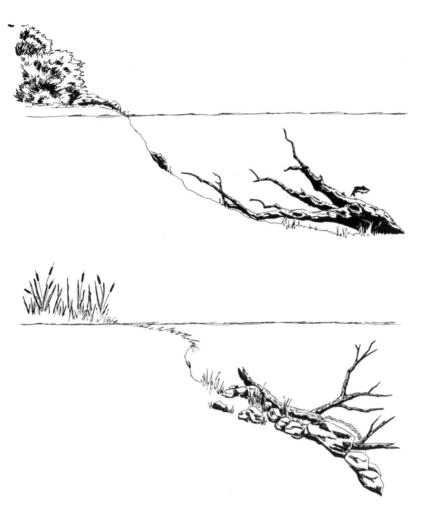

The shape and composition of a shoreline often give a fisherman clues to the adjacent bottom. But not always. In these two situations, there is not much visible to a fisherman that would indicate fish-holding structure. In situation illustrated at top, a fisherman would have some clue to the possibility of good fishing at times because of the obvious dropoff at shoreline, plus rocks. But unless the water was very clear or he discovered it later, the old tree would be a bonus surprise. In situation shown above, the seemingly slow drop along shore would fool the casual observer. During low water, one branch of the dead tree might be exposed, bringing a watchful fisherman in on a potential hotspot. Hidden structure like this is good reason for thoroughly exploring any lake you fish.

catch no fish near a few of these docks it's very easy to say, "Well the bass aren't holding by the docks today," and try elsewhere. Yet a fisherman who has worked the docks thoroughly, one by one, may know that the one at, say, the blue house over yonder, or the one you almost reached before quitting and running up the lake, has a deep gully just off the end of it that leads right into a major weedbed.

The misrepresentation that a top-water viewpoint can give is great. The hazard is bad enough when you're dealing with man-made cover. With natural cover on a natural lake, it's worse. It is this natural cover that gave me such a shock when I first began examining it at fisheye level.

Take, for instance, an innocent-looking tree that has toppled over on its side, its trunk and branches thrusting down through the water.

This fallen-down tree is an excellent roadway for bass on their ways to shoreline feeding. It is not thick enough to hold numbers of fish, but some largemouths may hold along its length. If they do so, the bass will be underneath the projection, their backs up almost touching the structure.

If you're like most bass fishermen, you'll ease up to such a deadfall, toss out a spinnerbait perhaps, let it drop, and crank it back along one side of the trunk. Then you'll do the same on the other side. Maybe you'll work your lure across in front, where the branches go down in a maze. If you're convinced something's really there, maybe you'll cast a worm or a plastic grub rigged weedless straight back along the trunk. You let the lure settle a little, then start hopping it or swimming it back. If you were fishing a tournament, you'd be gone by now. But maybe you're not. So you work that plastic bait through the branches some more, just to make sure you've covered it all. Nothing.

"He's not home," you say. You jam the rods back into their holders, yank back the electric, then fire up the big motor.

No, he wasn't home. But *they* were. If it was a good size tree and the main cover in the area, six, eight, or more bass could be in there. Depending on where you live, these fish could be big—6 pounds up into the teens!

Where are the bass? Back under that log, I mean really under it, with their dorsal fins practically stuck up against the trunk. They are not alongside it or over it or in the branches. They are *under* the cover. Because this tree angles downward from shore to the deeper water, they are facing toward the shore so they don't have to hold station with their noses down.

On your previous tries, your lures mainly went past at just about the level of the underside of the dead tree, which was about at bass-belly level. The worms and grubs dropped down to the bottom all right, on those casts where the line was not holding them up because it was hung on some stub or other. But when those plastic lures stopped sinking, you started them back almost immediately. They moved away from the main tree trunk and into the branches, where you gave them all sorts of pretty action, letting them snake around the limbs, then dropping them down again. The only trouble was that no bass were there.

How do I know this is what would happen? Very simply. I have asked a number of very good bass fishermen to work this typical downed-tree situation while I watched below.

"Fish it the best way you can," I asked them. "I think there may be a good bass in there." After such requests I would swim down and closely observe how their lures were presented. If I went into the water first and reported that several mighty bass were in that tree jungle, the fishermen would work at it much longer and much more carefully. But after a while they would begin to doubt my word. Then the quality of their presentation would drop off. How should you approach this situation? I'll detail tactics for these tight-cover situations one by one.

But now look at another location problem: the bass are in supercover, but you can't find them with your lures. I was skimming just over the bottom in 13 feet of water in a smallish Northeastern lake looking for fish. Visibility was about 12 feet. I was moving along the inside (shoreside) edge of a moss bed over which I had often found bass in positions that made for easy lure presentation. Today no fish were to be seen. There were no fish around or beneath the shoreline holding places where I often found them. It was beginning to worry me.

The contour of the moss bed turned slightly outward. As I passed over the point formed by this bend, I caught a movement just below and to the right at the edge of my vision. For most of my underwater observation work I now use a mask with side glass to get all the peripheral vision I can. With regular diving masks, most of our peripheral vision is lost. Underwater wildlife often chooses to make a telltale move as you are nearly past. Without side vision, I had really been working with blinders in the past. Had I not changed, I'd never have seen the giveaway movement on which I now was concentrating.

It was a bass. The fish rolled up from the moss as my shadow hovered over it. Then the bass fled into the depths to disappear behind a curtain of suspended particulate matter. It had been completely hidden in the moss. Now I began searching more carefully. At a small cut in the bed farther on, another bass waited until I had nearly passed before coming out to get a better look at the darkly ominous bubbling creature that I must have appeared. This one simply dropped down into the cover again as I moved away. I flipped over to face the place where he had vanished. Carefully dropping to the bottom, I inched forward on my fingertips. My finned feet stuck straight back, and I tried to puff up as little sediment as possible with them. It was as though this fish had constructed a cocoon around himself. His head was at the edge of the bed, his body back in the tunnel of vegetation. As I closed in, he shot off out of sight.

I found more fish similarly tunneled into low-growing vegetation this day and on subsequent dives. I also found bass in major weedbeds that grew from the bottom to within inches of the surface. They didn't merely hold at the edges of such weeds, where a lure can run enticingly. They withdrew into the very heart of the weedbeds—beds so thick that had I been on land I would have used a machete to chop my way through. What a thing to fish in! But it was the way they tunneled down out of sight even in the low vegetation that impressed me most.

How to convince such bass to attack a lure is what I had to work on—that and getting a lure to them in the first place. I was successful to a surprising degree. But again, before going into tactics we'd better look at one more case of supercover that needs to be cracked.

One of the very worst problems is a shoreline situation. I don't recommend that you study a favorite fishing bank underwater unless you promise yourself to continue bass fishing despite what you've seen. Very likely the seeming impossibility of the situation could tempt you never to fish the shore again.

A good bass angler knows the importance of casting his lures up tight to a bank in order to produce fish. Tight means an inch away, or certainly no more than 2 inches away; 3 or 4 inches from target and you might as well forget it. How can such a small distance matter that much? It's because of a misconception we've had for a long time about the nature of undercut banks and the way bass can use them to their advantage.

The terms *bankhole* and *undercut shoreline* really don't give a true picture of the labyrinths that extend far back beneath many banks. I've learned that mazelike undercutting occurs not only in the South but in the North as well, though not quite as consistently bad. The islands, mats, and main shorelines of Georgia grass in the South are probably the worst situations with which you'll have to deal. I remember the first time I became aware of what we are really up against as fishermen. I was finning along about 5 feet beneath the surface, 10 feet out from a shore of Georgia grass, in a

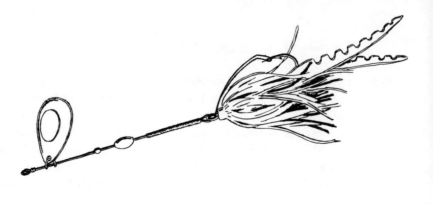

Some of the more effective weedless (but not fishless) swimming lures designed to fish supercover. These can be dredged over matts of vegetation and dropped into tiny pockets along the course of the retrieve.

Top to bottom: Snagless Sally; Subria weedless jig; Nympho. These lures can be put together from components you most likely now own.

The Snagless Sally is formed from a shaft spinner attached to a weedless (wireguard-type) hook. The hook is dressed with a skirt clear spring lake in central Florida. It was easy to look back into the root network of the grass and to spot the silhouettes of big largemouths hiding there in the shade. Light refraction causes underwater objects to seem closer and larger than they actually are. At first the bass didn't seem too far back in the cover. Then I happened to look up at what was the edge of the grass. *Those fish are back in there a ways,* I thought, but the roots and tricky light playing through them gave the appearance of looseness, a place where you could swim a spoon or a spinnerbait or crawl a worm. Then I surfaced.

I was closer to the edge of the grass than I thought. I ducked back under and moved right up to the edge of the grass. I tried to hold a mental picture of the nearest bass's location, allowing for the underwater magnification, then surfaced again. It was a shocker. The fish was back far deeper than I had thought possible. From the surface the grass was not a series of broken channels at all. Any lure cast upon it would sit there solidly. From then on, I began to examine the undercuts carefully.

In the North I learned that while entire shorelines might not be as deeply undercut as in the South, there were distinct holes that extended back into blackness. I remembered catching fish in some of these places in the past, though far from consistently.

Eventually I took an old metal tape rule down with me in a Southern lake. I measured undercuts where fish had been holding. They were alarming—8, 10, 16 feet back in! There were places

from a commercial spinnerbait (you may need to cement it into place) and a plastic lizard tail. A pork chunk could replace the plastic tail.

The Subria is a flathead jig with a curly-tail plastic lure on it. The weedguard is simply a piece of Mylar. Mylar is a tough film material with gold color on one side, silver on the other. It is available in fly-tying specialty shops in sheet form, from which such weedguards as shown here may be cut.

The Nympho is nothing more than a plastic worm hooked to a keel hook. The body is formed of latex wrapped around the hook. Stiff sections of monofilament tied in at the head make the hook even more weedless.

where the undercuts just seemed to keep going, as I'm sure the bass did when they desired. How far do you think such a fish, unless he is in an extremely positive feeding mood, will come from his secure holding station to smash your lure?

In many other situations you may not be reaching bass with lures presented in the normal fashion. Getting to the fish becomes a matter of changing your approach. In each place where the fish may be holding tightly in or under such supercover, it will pay to think the situation through carefully to determine whether or not some trick can be devised to make the proper presentation. These are situations in which normal lure presentations won't reach the fish.

Bass will squeeze into the tightest places for security. These three huge largemouths found good cover beneath support of a dock. They are practically unreachable in such situations unless they are in a positive feeding attitude. At such times, they may rush out at a lure presented close to their lair.

I have found bass in the crumbling remains of old bridge supports where, if your line or lure didn't snag, current would certainly sweep the hooked lure or bait away before it could work into the strike zone. Many times I've located largemouths holding beneath large moored boats or barges. The bigmouths would station themselves almost touching the hulls with their backs. While exploring the rotting timbers of old cribbings that once supported one type of building or other structure, I've nearly swallowed my scuba mouthpiece when a thick-bodied bass emerged from some darkened crevice that was effectively protected by crossbeams and debris from all penetration by normally presented lures.

By no means are these cover-tight bass loners. Shallow-water in-cover bass are just as likely to be in small to quite good-size schools as open-water bass. Not all the bass in a given school will be the same size, though the smaller fish are more frequently grouped with similar individuals. In a group of ten or twelve big fish, you may find bass ranging from 6 to maybe 13 pounds. It is the larger more aggressive (with one another) fish that take possession of the heaviest or best cover.

Knowing this, you might just as well go to the thickest section first when you fish in difficult places. You can then be practically sure that you're working for the largest bass of the bunch.

By now, I have many times observed this behavior of the larger fish taking possession of the better places. I have seen it along fallen trees, beneath undercut banks, and in weedbeds. If similar cover exists in an area, there will still be spots (though we may not be able to see it) that have a little something extra that makes them preferable. The bigger fish will take these, and bass of slightly lesser rank will be quite close to them. In fact, in prime heavy cover, even the larger bass often bunch like sardines.

I have seen one fish in a preferred spot swim off for one reason or another. Quite soon a bass that had been holding close—a bass of probably the same size—will shift into the position held by the first. The first bass, upon returning, will swim alongside the other fish in the group until he reaches the position he first occupied. Once there, he will push himself back into holding station. The second bass—along with others that may have closed ranks—will move aside for him. After observing a group long enough, it was possible to identify most of its members through specific marks, old injuries, and—in several cases—tags. Therefore it was possible to confirm

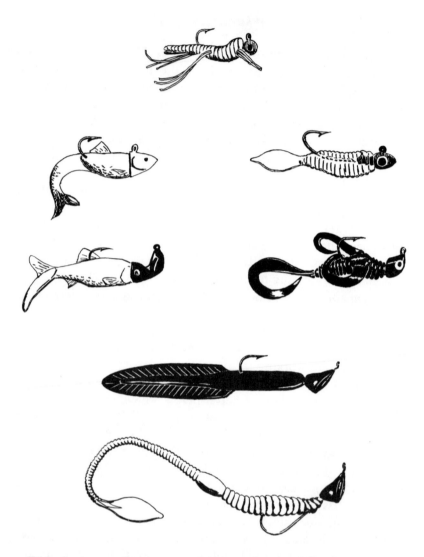

With the innovation of various plastic tails, the common bucktail jig is given a new lease on life. Ensuing lure is called a grub, plastic minnow, eel, or salamander—depending on the tail dressing used—and is among the most effective bass lures. It should be used more often by fishermen. It has a place in cover that will not constantly foul the exposed hook. Clockwise from top: Ugly Bug with rubber legs; Stingray grub; Mr. Twister salamander; Pow-RR jig head with eel; Pow-RR head rigged with worm in weedless fashion; Vibro-Tail jig; Wig-Wag Minnow.

which bass returned. Occasionally a bass would merely circle away from the group, remain in sight, and then return.

There is no fighting, but I have seen a returning bass move slowly to his place and flare his gills several times as though to make sure the others knew who was boss. I wondered why there was never any fighting among the big bass in these situations.

Rudolph Miller of Oklahoma State University has a feasible answer: Bass, while young, engage in display movements such as biting, chasing, and butting under natural conditions. Dr. Miller believes that the youngsters learn from such activity to estimate the size and potential strength of their fellows as they grow. As mature adults, they can use this estimating ability without resorting to combat. Just to make sure there is no confusion over who is top fish, the larger bass often enforce their position through so-called assertive displays such as the gill flaring that I observed when the bass jockeyed for preferred positions in the limited space of prime heavy cover.

It doesn't matter whether a choice heavy cover is shallow or deep. Bass use it for two reasons: (1) security during nonfeeding periods, and (2) ambushing purposes when they are in a positive (feeding) attitude.

The phenomenon of where bass are in heavy cover was reduced to its essence by tournament veteran Billy Phillips of Jackson, Tennessee. "Largemouths like cover they can get under," said Billy. "If that kind of cover plus food are present, you don't have to have a lot of fancy sonar gear and oxygen meters to know there are bass around."

Finding them is usually more than half the battle, but that's not always true in supercover. Jimmy Houston, the Bass Anglers Sportsman Society's (B.A.S.S.) 1976 Angler of the Year, had something to say on the matter.

"People don't realize what percentage of the time they just absolutely do not have a chance of catching a fish," insisted the Tahlequah, Oklahoma, angler.

I'd paraphrase Jimmy's statement like this: People don't realize what percentage of the time they're just not putting their lures where and how the fish want them.

"My cardinal rule," Jimmy Houston hastily added, "is to fish the heaviest shallow-water cover I can find, and preferably with deep water nearby."

All well and good, but how do you present your lures to the fish in some of these "impossible" places?

Tactics

No one said it would be easy. To fish the supercover effectively, you need, as the Irish say, the patience of a saint. You also need:
- the control and reflexes of an in-trim athelete,
- equipment in perfect working order, and
- a willingness to change your preferred approaches.

If you have none of these attributes, you ought to give the heavy cover a try anyway from time to time. If you do, eventually something very large and mean and tough is going to clamp down on your lure. Once that happens—regardless of the outcome of the battle—you just may wind up a supercover angler for life.

The toughest yet potentially most productive situations with which you'll consistently have to deal include those places I've just discussed: (1) timber mazes, (2) fish tunneled in low vegetation, (3) bass in thick weedbeds, and (4) deep undercuts. From the preceding section, you should know about where the fish will be. The problem is how to achieve a proper presentation to lure the bass into taking. Let's look at each situation separately.

Timber

Regular timber is not so much of a problem. It's the interwoven mazes, which provide bass places to really get far under, that make for a supercover situation. As you saw earlier, a normally presented lure usually is not going to draw them out.

Not too long ago a fine California bass angler by the name of Dee Thomas adapted for modern equipment, the ancient art of canepole fishing for bass. His technique, dubbed *flippin'*, is one that a flycaster would learn very quickly. Here are the steps: (1) strip an arm's length of line from a bait-casting reel, (2) hold that line in your left hand, and (3) use an underhand rod flip to send a weedless jig out to target. As the lure is flipped, your left hand moves, feeding the reel-free line through the guides. The lure shoots out on a low trajectory and enters the water gently. Once it hits water, the jig is allowed to fall vertically on a slightly slack line. Dee then commences to swim the jig back by raising and lowering his rod, which is quite long for a casting rod. Each time the lure hits an obstruction, it is made to climb over and then permitted to fall vertically once again. The Thomas method is based on the premise that a tightly holding bass is not in a mood to chase a lure very far. Therefore he must hold his jig right on cover.

He is right.

I have found through underwater observation, however, that even this slow up-and-down, crawl-over-and-drop retrieve may not be holding the lure in front of the bass long enough when they're completely beneath a wide section of timber. When the fish are really being difficult, they may display initial interest; then when the lure eases away even slightly, they go back to dreaming whatever it is that they dream about when not thinking of chasing dinner.

Would a different kind of lure have worked better? No. The simple lead head unencumbered by spinners gives you precise control. It sinks quickly on the spot and can be held at any depth. The small jig is perfect for this kind of situation. The trick is to work this lure so it remains hovering beside the thickest section of cover until you just cannot stand it any more, or until your arm gives out. The long bait-casting rod Dee Thomas uses is ideal for such a tactic.

If you are not in a tournament where rod length is limited, a stout canepole with its extra length can be a further advantage. Old-timers who tied a lure or natural bait inches below the tip end of an 18-foot pole and worked their plugs or spoons in figure eights, splattering and bubbling the water with the cane tip, knew the effectiveness of keeping a lure on station longer. The method was called jiggerpoling, and it took a lot of bass. Still, the noisy approach often resulted in refusals when the fish were especially sensitive.

The ideal method is to approach quite close to the cover. You can move in as close as 10 feet, maybe 7. To get that close it is best to take advantage of a breeze or current coming from the right direction. Anchor your boat, and then let out anchor line until your boat drifts on station. You must remain deathly quiet. Respected nature-film producer Glen Lau established that bass have a built-in alert zone with a radius of about 15 feet. Within that sphere, the fish are keenly aware of everything. Lau's observations are accurate. In extremely calm weather or if the sun is likely to throw the shadow of you and your boat over probable holding stations of bass, do *not* attempt to stalk as close as I've just suggested. Be aware of possible shadows from your arm, body, and rod.

The underhand flipping cast is best for your presentation. Send the smallest jig you can handle out low to plop alongside the thickest section of cover. Allow it to drop below the timber and simply hover. Your arm should be extended fully unless the shadow of your rod would fall across the bass's line of vision. Even then, unless you're using a long canepole, or the wind-driven current is moving toward the cover to hold your line and lure in position, the jig will slowly swim to place below your rod tip. While it is swimming, impart a gentle series of up-and-down vibrations to the lure. When the jig has reached the end of its swim beneath your rod, hold it there. From time to time jiggle it gently.

An alternative method is to allow the jig to settle to the bottom on a fairly slack line once it enters the water. Then slowly raise your rod tip, vibrating the lure slightly. Immediately drop the jig again to the bottom. Do this several times. Then raise your rod higher and jig the lure. Now hold the lure suspended, so it gently swims back toward your rod. Finally, pluck your jig softly from the water for another flip back at the entry point. Repeat this maneuver over and over again. You will be covering an area of only a very few feet, thus keeping your lure in the likely fish-holding area much longer than you would if you completed a full retrieve from a greater distance. This is what is needed to entice the nonactive bass into hitting. The small jig is vital. Casting over and over with a spinner or plug would normally put the fish off.

Gear yourself up mentally to focus on the slightest movement of line or jig. If your concentration wanders, which can happen very easily, you will likely miss the fleeting moment of a take. The bass are so close to the lure that they have to move little (if at all) to take it. The small jig makes even tougher your task of detecting an easy take.

From an underwater vantage point, I have watched how skilled bass anglers jig for some time in such situations. Often a very large bass would indicate its excitement by rapid in-place fin movement. He would slowly, stiffly turn, face the lure, and in the wink of an eye flare his gills. The movement causes a suction like that of the slurp gun used by divers to collect small swimming fish. The jig would disappear into the mouth of the bass. But in a moment the bass would spew it out again. The fishermen would insist that he never felt or saw a thing. The fish, however, don't always get away with that business.

There will be plenty of times when you'll detect the take— usually when the line twitches. When you do, you must strike jet-fast and in the same motion keep pulling on that rod, Sweeping the fish away from the jungle. From watching hooked bass underwater, I can safely say that the first reaction of your hooked fish will probably be to flee for deeper water. The nearest route to deeper water will most likely be through more of that timber maze, so you must strive to sweep the fish from the cover immediately. If he cannot make the deeper water, your fish will veer right back into the densest cover to bury himself, or at least his front end. Keep these predictable reactions in mind and you'll be primed to counter them when they occur.

The kind of approach I've just described is all it takes to pluck big largemouths from dense timber. You bet it is tough. Would you like to try something easier? How about a situation where you can use some well-learned casting skill?

Vegetation

You may have absolutely no trouble catching bass when they're active and higher up in weeds, or along the shoreward or deep-water edge of a weedbed. During those periods, bass are very likely to dart out from the ambush points to grap a spinner or plug that happens by. But far too often the fish aren't there.

Earlier I told about locating bass buried in cocoon-like tunnels of moss. As I spent more and more time underwater, I found the fish burrowed in other types of vegetation as well. They were hunkered down in pockets where cabbage weed—that tall weed with broad leaves—was giving over to low eelgrass. I found them, too, dug in at the bottom of the trunk network of coontail weed, the thick, many-branched vegetation that reaches to the surface and umbrellas outward as it grows higher.

When the fish are down and under vegetation, there are two good ways you can fish for them: (exposed-hook jigs or weedless worms and jigs.)

(1) I first try plastic grubs or worms with wiggly, curly-type tails rigged with an exposed-hook jighead. If I can get by without hanging weeds on my hook constantly, I prefer to fish this way. It eliminates having to sink my hook past a weedguard or through plastic.

You'd be surprised how some of the jighead designs enable you to literally rip your lure right through some varieties of weeds. Often bass will strike after the lure rips free. I no longer sharply jig these plastic-tail-and-lead-head lures, because I've seen how the fish respond to a lot of different retrieves.

The best retrieve in this situation is a simple swimming along, over the low weeds. What you do is raise your rod slightly, then slowly lower it as you swim-crawl the jighead lure along. Then you pause only a brief moment to allow your lure to settle. Raise your rod tip and ease the rig along a few more inches; then let it settle again. You'll be pulling the lure through weeds, so you must develop in your touch a sense of when resistance is simply vegetation and when it is a bass that has engulfed the lure. This technique is successful when the fish are lying in pockets in the vegetation. I also bring them out of their moss tunnels using it, if I can manage to keep that green algae from fouling my hook. The only way to accomplish that is to eliminate the settling portion of the retrieve. What I do is swim the lure, then pause, letting the wormjig just hang for an instant before starting the swim again.

When you must deal with separate clumps of a weedlike coontail or cabomba, you'll have to use one of the triangular-shaped or spear-type jigheads. Because this is not a solid-weedbed type of situation, you'll be able to cast over a clump, let the wormjig settle,

Supercover—weeds style. Many anglers will consider and then pass by such areas because they experience fouled lures. However, many times the bass are in the heart of such aquatic thickets. A weedless spoon, or a spinnerbait buzzed on top, will often bring the fish up. The other technique is to work the edges of such weed.

then bring it back through the vegetation. Hop it back gently, not sharply. Then when you hit the main body of the weeds, you'll have to rip the hook through. Stand by for a strike when you do, for the fish are holding down around the trunk of this weed growth, and the struggling lure causes them to become very excited.

I have watched such a jig come through the weeds underwater. And though from my position I could not always see the fish, as soon as the lure broke free a bass was on it like a cat that has finally decided to make its all-out charge upon a barn mouse.

(2) When you begin dealing with the large and truly thick weedbeds, you must go with one sort of weedless terminal rig or another. You can use the standard Texas sliding-sinker rig on a plastic worm, with the hook buried in plastic. Lately I've taken to pegging the sliding sinker in place against the plastic worm with a bit of toothpick when I'm working in brush, and I've carried the practice over in weed fishing. It prevents the problem of having the sinker fall on one side of an obstruction while the worm hangs on the other. There are also some excellent relatively new worm weights with metal eyes in each end. You can rig these in two ways:

· The most popular method is to open the rear sinker eye with pliers, clip on your hook, close the eye, and put on the worm in the usual way.

· The other way to use the weights is to thread your line through the forward sinker eye, then out through the rear sinker eye. Then you tie the line to the hook. If you use line of about 12-pound test or more, this rigging permits the sinker to slide but not as freely as with the center-hole weight.

Another way to rig weedlessly is to use hooks with weedguards. The easiest way to use such hooks is to insert the point in the center of the worm head and run it down and out the side of the worm about one-half to three-quarters inch below the head. The eye of the hook must remain out of the worm head because of the wire weedguard.

Bobby Martin, a fine bass fisherman from Springfield, Missouri, showed me a technique for rigging a weedless hook with the eye inside the worm. This is how to do it: First tie your line on the hook. Next insert the barb on the side of the worm about one-quarter inch below the head instead of up front in the center of the head. Run the point down inside the worm about one one-quarter to one one-half an inch and then out. Now slide the worm up the shank until you reach the weedguard. The hook eye is then inserted into the hole that you made when you inserted the point the first time. Push the eye and hook collar in and forward toward the head. The line, which will be on the side of the worm, is then pulled so it cuts its way to the center of the worm head. The plastic will close over the cut.

Finally, most of the jigheads previously described can be rigged in weedless fashion. The way to do it successfully is to insert the point in the center of the worm head and bring it out after running it no more than three-eighths inch down the worm body. Turn the hook around and imbed the point into the worm body, as you do when using the standard Texas rig.

A new jig type has a spur extending from the head. You simply push the worm over the spur, then embed the barb in the worm body. It's a super rig.

Many times anglers approach heavy weed cover, try a few casts, and discover that they can't even get their lures down. Normal casting in such cover generally results in having the lures supported by the tops of truly thick weeds, whether of the tall cabbage type of the overhanging canopies of coontail. On the retrieve, great fist-size clots of vegetation collect around the head of the lure. Certainly during times when the bass have stationed themselves just below a weed canopy, they will break through to engulf lures struggling in the mat. But too often the fish are down. These deeper-lying fish are the ones that present the most difficulty, and so I went below again to gain a bass-eye view of the situation.

It is a strange, mysterious feeling probing the depths of the underwater jungles. It is also a fascinating experience. Populations of panfish, boldly curious and secure in the safety of such cover, approach close enough for you to touch. The only inhabitants of this weedy world that I did not relish meeting were the thick-bodied snapping turtles. I never enjoyed them on the surface, and underwater they would lurk, thrust out their evil-looking heads, and stare before scooting off. They never gave me any trouble, but just the same I didn't like them.

The bass in these jungles were often down on the bottom or suspended deep in the weeds. As I looked up, I found more openings in the mat than I had expected. Still, on the surface the situation was tighter than it was below. At the top, the weeds tended to branch out; they could no longer grow straight up. If you could get your lures down past the umbrella, you'd probably have a chance.

I found that as a diver I had to ease my way slowly through the ropes of cabbage or beneath the coontail parasols. Over-enthusiastic movements caused me to become entangled, just as frantically worked lures would hang up. I had discovered my first clue to fishing deep in the aquatic jungles.

I began experimenting with the weedless worm rigs earlier described. Underwater, I would try to wait at the edge of the weedlines to avoid frightening the bass that were holding inside. I asked the anglers who were in the boat above to make pinpoint casts to the small open pockets they could locate, and then to let their lures sink before beginning any kind of retrieve. Initially I saw that the straight jigging or hopping retrieves would sometimes generate interest. Very often the lures would be followed by a bass. Where there were openings, I could often see the fish following as the lures worked through. Then the bass would slowly turn away. These fish could have easily nailed the worms but were obviously not in a chasing mood. Perhaps the lures were just not spending enough time near the fish. Perhaps an even slower, teasing retrieve would work.

What I finally came up with was a variation on the retrieve used successfully in the thick timber situations. To execute it, cast your worm to the small open pockets, allow it to settle, and then pulsate it in place so that the tail waves gently. The use of standup-type jigheads with the hook weedlessly imbedded into the worm helps you achieve this action.

After you make the lure vibrate in place, pump the worm up slowly and crawl it lightly over the weed tops until it reaches a new pocket. At this point, you let the worm drop. Let it rest for a few moments. Then gently dance the lure in place before beginning the lift again. You will need a weight or head of up to one-half ounce in the thickest vegetation, though three-eighths ounce is preferable if it is enough to sink the lure through the vegetation. For this kind of fishing I like worms 4 to 6 inches long.

Observing below the surface at the edges of the weeds, I noticed something: Although this method was very often successful, the bass would sometimes follow slowly quite some distance without taking. If such a fish were going to hit at all, he would usually do it the instant the lure snapped into clear water from the weedbed. I suppose he figured the imitation was about to escape. You can capitalize on this behavior by allowing your lure to drop freely just as it breaks out of the weeds. Usually the bass will hit on this drop. If he does not, dance the lure a few moments on the bottom before you crank it in.

As in the heavy-timber situation, you must position your boat quite close to the area you'll be fishing. You'll also have to make small shifts in the boat placement to properly cover all the potential pockets in a promising weedbed. If you fish from shore or wade, plan your casts before making them. Adjust your location to make the best presentations. It was once thought that getting so close would put the fish off. When bass are in the kind of weeds

Precise boat positioning is important in catching bass. Electric motors or pushpoles go a long way to help in fine manipulation of craft. Here author poles his son toward point of lilypad matt. Such isolated cover is often better than primary shore cover.

we've been discussing, and if you move slowly and quietly, you will neither spook them nor cause them to refuse to strike.

There is one final supercover situation for which you should be prepared. This is the one I had to prove to myself with a tape measure.

Bankholes and Undercuts

When I took that rollup ruler below to measure just how far back some of the undercut banks of the Georgia grass went, I'll admit to some nervousness: the same kind of nervousness you get when thinking about what might drop on you while you work cypress trees in a boat. You know the stories about cottonmouths or other snakes dropping into a boat. As I swam up to those overhanging, undershot shorelines and approached the dark caverns that extended far back out of sight, I had visions of all manner of undesirable creatures slithering out to greet me. I never had a snake problem, though there were times when those big eelish Southern salamanders known as sirens gave me a start.

Back in these undercuts and bankholes, I found some of the largest bass I've ever seen underwater. Often because the cover was in shadow, I would move in too close and spook a fish, which would explode from his den. The suddennness of the action and the glimpse of huge shapes would set my heart pounding, and I'd gulp compressed air wastefully. Sometimes I could see the backlighted silhouettes of largemouths—deep-bodied with massively undershot jaws—far in beneath the roots of grass. At other times, illumination came from the open-water side, where I was.

When I saw light showing the bass in silhouette, I realized the light was coming from somewhere other than the lake behind me. It was the first clue that there might be a way to get a lure near these fish.

This backlight proved to be filtering down through occasional breaks in the surface of grass. The surface was much like a bog or marsh. You can walk on and on upon solid ground; then, without warning, you plunge knee-deep into water. I investigated further and found that some of these breaks were woven over with vegetation, but with water showing between the basket patterns of the grasses. Other breaks were clearer. Between these openings and the main bank was fairly solid grass mat.

The technique I began to use in this situation has proven itself, especially where the breaks or openings in the grass are not too far from the bank. What we did was position a boat directly in front of the opening, then cast tandem spinnerbaits or shaft spinners with weedless hooks, skirt, and pork chunk inland over the bank to the far end of the break. Then we'd start the weed-shucking lure churning and clanking over the opening to inform any fish present that something, maybe dinner, was fast approaching.

If you kept up the momentum, the spinnerbait would not snag. Instead, it would skim across the grass. When you reached the edge of the bank, you simply let the lure drop and flutter down. If nothing happened we'd hold the boat in place and start cranking the lure fast—no fancy hops or jigging action needed. I have had bass smash the lure both on the drop at the bank edge and when I began the retrieve. Some grasses will present more of a problem than others, trapping your lure in tough V's of stalk. But where the technique can be managed, it can produce fish.

There is another method that developed during attempts to coax out any bass that would move from his cavern-like hole or undercut hideout. It involved moving your boat close to shore near a known sanctuary. What you do is cast parallel and tight to the bank past the hole. Then you bring your lure back past the hideout. Depending on how deep you need to fish, you can use a tandem or single-blade spinnerbait, or any of the curly-tail worms. If definite holding stations are not known, you can always move along with an electric motor, positioning yourself so that your retrieves run as close as possible along the more promising-looking shore.

Variations on this game include one method practiced by bank fishermen who, over the years, have learned the whereabouts of the deeper undercuts. Using long poles or rods, they stay pretty far back from the shoreline. They move into position as carefully as any angler stalking a brown trout in a limestone creek, for they know they're probably treading over places where a bass is hiding. These fishermen flip out small jigs or natural baits—both on floats. The keep their offerings very close to the edge of the bank. If they use a leadhead jig, they'll keep the lure barely swimming and dancing in front of the better holds. Natural baits are just permitted to float. If live baits are used they must be tended, moving them back into position if they swim out too far, or pulling them out if they swim back very far beneath the banks. Should a bass take a bait many feet back under, you'll have a difficult time extracting him.

I've seen some of these bank fishermen just at the time a grandma-size largemouth came shooting from beneath the grass and grabbed their lure. One moment the fisherman would be quietly standing there working his long rod and looking like some long-legged bird—a heron, perhaps. The next instant the rod would be U-bent and the angler holding on with both hands.

Another effective method for bringing big bass from beneath the undercuts is worked from the water side. Here, too, live bait is used. The favorite baits in the South for this method are huge native golden shiners or large salamanders. In the North, live nightcrawlers or smaller shiners native to the area are employed. Outfitter John D. McClanahan and guide Porter Hall have honed this method to perfection. These men, among the many who practice this specialty fishing, work the tactic primarily in central Florida, but it's just as deadly anywhere in the country where bass can get far back under the banks. They specialize in luring trophy-size Florida bass out from hiding with shiners up to 11 inches long!

When you're fishing in the North or for smaller-size bass, you must scale down the tackle. For his method, John likes a short-shank 3/0 to 8/0 Wright & McGill Model 84 hook. The eye and first ½ inch of shank are bent at a 45-degree angle toward the point. On the hook go two tiny disks or washers, which may be stamped from plastic or rubber. The minnow is lip-hooked. One disk goes on before the bait is hooked; the other goes on after. These act as stoppers, helping to keep the hook in the proper position when the bait swims around and is moved back on station. The disks also help prevent the hook from riding around and hooking into the bait rather than the bass when the strike is made.

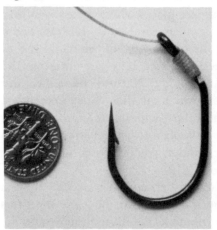

A customized bass hook (left) is used by John McClanahan of Orange Springs, Florida. John bends the hook to the shape shown to give a better direction of pull when hook is set. McClanahan also has a technique of using small rubber disks on either side of a shiner's lips (right) when fishing this live bait. The little washers help prevent hook from circling around and rehooking the bait instead of the bass when hook is set.

To get slightly different action, John sometimes eliminates the disks, and hooks the bait behind the dorsal. Frequently the shiners are fin-clipped to cause them to move erratically. Slip bobbers are used to keep the bait at the proper depth.

McClanahan and Hall are after the largest, most difficult fish, so they want everything possible in their favor. They rarely use artificials. Working with long, custom-made rods and revolving-spool bait-casting reels, they cast their baits close to the banks toward any little cut that might indicate a hole or channel that runs far beneath the grass.

The big bass generally cannot resist baits of the size John and Porter offer them. Eventually, even the most wary move out from their dens to take. At this point the method is very exacting. You must place the reel into free-spool while the bass moves with the bait. The big bass pull even large bobbers under as they swim with the bait. Only experience can tell you when to strike. You cannot wait too long, nor can you strike too quickly. First of all, however, you must be sure you're within 40 or 45 feet of the fish. John and Porter mark their lines with waterproof felt pens so they know they are within the proper distance. If you strike with much more monofilament than that out, you stand a good chance of losing your fish because of line stretch.

What the two trophy hunters do is lift anchor and follow the bass if he begins moving off with the bait. They follow, using an electric motor, giving line if the fish moves faster, taking line in as they can. When the magic distance mark appears at the rod tip, they crank just a little more until they begin to feel the weight of the fish. Then, rod low, they sweep back in an arcing strike with all the power they can muster.

If you try this technique, those cat-and-mouse, give-and-take moments when you're following a huge bass and trying to close the distance to striking range can be some of the most nerve-racking that you will ever experience. But the technique is a winner. If you stick with it, I can safely say that one day you'll surely lure the kind of bass that dreams are made of and that it will come from so far beneath a bank that nonfishing folks may at one time have had a family picnic above his head. And that's what fishing supercover is like.

2

How Weather Affects Bass

Two kinds of weather must be considered in any fishing: (1) the seasonal weather, and (2) the short-term trends within each season.

As far as bass are concerned, the most important myth-stomper about weather is this: Contrary to popular belief, after spring spawning is completed and the fish have settled into normal routines, you can expect to find various bass populations at *all* primary depth levels all at the same time.

What this means is that it's no longer good enough to say, "Well, the fish are up tight in the bushes today," just because you caught a few there. In a little while those bush-oriented bass will very probably turn off, and the ones floating over, say, an old stone wall in 17 feet of water will start to feed.

Don't those deeper fish have to move in to the shallows to eat? No. Not if forage is nearby, which it probably will be. For a long time it has been convenient for fishermen to believe that all bass moved from deep to shallow water when it was dinner time. Sometimes the bass act this way, but not with the consistency we've always thought.

During the same day in the same lake, I've observed separate bass populations that fed at the surface near sunken islands, in the mid-depths off long sloping points, under gnarled-root networks of huge dead trees, out on reefs, and near various other areas. The depths varied from the surface to 20 feet down.

The feeding periods occurred at different times at various

depths. I wondered why. I found that although the air weather might be consistent, the underwater weather was composed of temperatures that varied approximately 20 degrees depending on the depth. It's well known that the cold-blooded bass is affected by the temperature of his surroundings. Here might be the reason for the varying feeding patterns. The bass at each depth fed at different times. The bass that fed in shallower water didn't necessarily feed more frequently than the deep-water bass, but the shallow-water bass usually consumed more during one feeding period. I couldn't ask a group of fish why they chose to hold at one level instead of another. I could only assume that for the time being they were content with the cover and the available forage. I also learned that a "home territory" is not permanent. The progression of seasons, and weather changes within a season, influenced relocation. I'm sure other factors, such as reduction of prey in a particular spot, also came into play.

Bass anglers like to talk of "patterns" in describing the situations in which they catch fish. For example, an angler may catch his fish near green brush, wood pilings, stickups, or a certain kind of point. The possibilities are nearly endless.

It would be far better, for instance, if a fisherman first made a survey of the potential shallow-water spots, those of only as much as 5 feet deep. Then he should locate possible holding places at middle depths (those of about 10 feet deep). Finally he can mark the deep holding structure, from 15 feet down. Remember that although the attractive cover or structure might be deep, the fish can be quite high over it. With probable hot spots now located, you are in a better position to take advantage of real patterns.

Do it by alternately working potential holding places in each of the three depth ranges instead of merely running from one cover to another in the same depth range. If a shallow-water pattern isn't working, why continue to hammer away when the water weather clock may be sounding the dinner gong for fish in another depth range?

Now consider some other myths about seasonal bass behavior.

There is still a school of thinking that says bass populations, because they are renewable, will continue to replenish themselves if we just fish and otherwise keep a hands-off policy. Fishing techniques are becoming more effective, and unfortunately fishing still means *keeping* to far too many bass anglers. Really dedicated bass fishermen have long ago seen the light, however, and are turning back their catch—often right on the spot, as do many anglers for stream trout.

The renewability of a bass resource is subject to fluctuations just as grain crops are—especially when no management techniques are applied. A bad springtime that lures the fish into spawning with freak warm periods, then turns alternately cold and warm, can play havoc with that year's class of young bass. The adult largemouths will leave the nests if the weather turns sour. This move sometimes happens before egg laying can take place. If the cold continues, eggs will be absorbed by the female. If spawning has taken place, a sudden cold snap can drive the guardian male bass into deeper water. If he stays away too long, the eggs will not receive their protective fanning. Sediment will accumulate and suffocate them. Fungus spores can attack them. A poor year class will not be noticed by most anglers, of course, until the time when the yearling fish that aren't there should be starting to provide sport.

Seasons

There's another widely held belief that in spring, once the weather shows promise, bass move directly from their winter lairs onto the spawning flats. In reality, before the nesting activity ever begins, bass have moved up or in as the case may be. In areas that have no established fishing seasons, anglers who have figured out this early movement often enjoy more sport than their colleagues who wait for warmer weather.

The first bass action usually occurs toward the north side of a small lake or cover, regardless of where the spawning grounds are located. This is so because the warming rays of the sun (which is located farther south at this time) will fall for a longer period on these nothern areas. There are local exceptions, of course, but pre-spawn holding places such as feeder creeks, cover with a good dropoff nearby, or an old submerged creek channel will prove most attractive during this early period if they receive benefit of the sun. When the water has warmed sufficiently, bass will work around to the shallows for spawning.

Summer brings a time when some water gets almost as warm as the air. Fishermen have named this period the doldrums and sometimes have trouble catching bass then. The truth is that usually the fishermen, not the fish, are in the doldrums. Anglers are often not willing to change from their springtime tactics. Techniques tailored to hot weather must be applied during summer dog days, and these will be discussed in the section "Hot-Weather Environment." For now, take heart that knowledgeable bass anglers can indeed enjoy wonderful summer sport.

Autumn is an interesting season for bass anglers. As the weather cools, anglers who never caught on to the summer "patterns" often find the bass biting again, for a time. Gradually, as the water grows cooler, those same anglers will find the action tapering off. "Bass have gone hibernating" is the favorite excuse. But they haven't. Three major movements and relocation migrations occur with the progression of autumn, and it is vital for dedicated bass enthusiasts to be aware of them.

First, as surface water cools, it gets heavier and drops through layers of warmer water beneath it. The warmer water in turn is forced up. This upwelling phenomenon is widely discussed by anglers. It's known as lake turnover. What it means to your fishing is this: Bass can now visit areas that may have been closed off to them just a few weeks earlier by low oxygen content in the water. The turning of the lake mixes a new supply of oxygen into deep water. The bass, released from the sometimes restricted movements of summer, now scatter widely. Where they go depends largely on where their prey moves.

Some forms of bass prey—threadfin and gizzard shad, for example—feed by extracting plant and other organic matter from mud. They strain the organisms from the mud with their gill rakers. More highly oxygenated water permits the little shad to expand their activities, and the bass follow.

• The second major bass movement in autumn involves a return to shallower water, though not necessarily right up to the banks. The young of shiners and shad, spawned in midsummer, have matured to tempting size by autumn. The bass find that these young forage fish begin moving from thick weeds and ultra-shallow water in order to satisfy their own foraging needs. The bass move in close enough to prey on these fish.

This is the time when bass often locate on shallow-water structure that's 20 to 60 feet from shore. They make periodic forays in to shore, but they also feed near the holding stations. Soon they will begin moving to their deeper wintering spots.

• In late autumn the third relocation movement begins. With ever-increasing cold, bass start drifting to the deep sunken creek beds, standing timber, or steep-walled shorelines, where they'll spend the winter. The misunderstanding about this period is the belief that bass move en masse to their cold-weather locations when a magic temperature is reached. It doesn't happen that way. In fact, what does happen is often the cause of great confusion among anglers.

What occurs is an uneven migration. Some bass will move to the sharp dropoffs used for winter sanctuaries, while other bass in the same lake are still making forays from moderately shallow offshore structure. In each of these locations, the fish will be influenced by local short-term conditions. It becomes confusing because you'll have two factors influencing the fish—the seasonal trend and the short-term trend.

The only thing to do during the late-fall period is alternately work both location types. You'd think that if the bass are feeding in winter locations, then the shallower-holding fish certainly must be feeding. But this is not always true. I've experienced days when the shallower fish were just sulking while the bass I found deep, just over a submerged creek bed, for example, were really tearing things up.

Late fall is an erratic time. There'll be days when you'll go fishless and others when you can do no wrong. Nothing's consistent this time of year. The best advice is to hit the water as often as possible, even in foul weather. The more you go, the better your chances for hitting either the shallow-water stragglers or the early snowbird bass in a feeding period before the truly dreadful weather sets in.

Weather Trends

Within the framework of overall seasonal influence, short-term weather trends have great effect upon bass behavior. To the best of my knowledge, no fishing forecast—whether based on sun and moon phases or on the result of computer readouts—has been able to compensate for these short-term trends. No generalized statement concerning seasonal fish behavior can encompass the varied influences of localized weather trends. Fishing forecasts tend to emphasize the importance of one or two particular phases of weather while discounting others. Some popular predictors discredit the importance of wind, for instance. Others emphasize only sun and moon position. Local short-term weather trends include factors such as shallow-water temperature, wind, light, storms, oxygen, and so on. All these elements work within the seasonal influence, and together they determine probable fishing success or lack of it on a day-to-day basis.

Much lore about localized short-term weather has sprung up. A lot of it is fanciful. Some has sound basis. However, rigid adherence to sweeping general statements on weather—even those based on truth—will cause you to miss out on some fine fishing. For instance, how about cold fronts? Hasn't it been proven that such weather trends send bass deep and stop their feeding? If you buy that notion entirely, you're eventually going to stop fishing anytime a cold snap occurs. That would be a shame.

First of all a frontal system must last for several days to affect fish behavior. One- or two-day systems, though very obvious to you, rarely alter bass behavior seriously. It usually takes a system of longer than three days to produce drastic changes in bass behavior. However, the first day of even a short-term front does usually produce some reaction. The effect is not a sudden disappearance of bass into heavy cover or their descent into deep water where they refuse to feed.

The most interesting effect occurs at the start of a sudden weather change after a period of fairly stable warm, sunny weather. You become extremely aware of the change if you have been watching bass in their natural environment day after day for some time. I found that with regular observation I was able to learn the routines of various bass populations quite well. I learned to distinguish individual fish with unusual markings, tags, and in some cases outstanding body configurations. Keeping tabs on those easily identifiable, I learned the territory they were using. Therefore I quickly became aware of any changes in the specific section of underwater world I had been observing.

I first saw the influence of sudden weather in a small clear lake with excellent visibility. It was springtime, and we had been having a period of shirtsleeve weather. Then one night it turned markedly cooler. When I dipped below the surface, the loner resident bass I always passed at the end of a little weedy point just off my entry point was gone. *I'll bet they're all deep,* I thought, swimming farther out.

There was usually a loose school of six fish patrolling just a little way from the weed point, and they weren't there either. Then I saw what looked like that group off to my left in a fairly shallow cove. They were moving, not far from the bottom, angled with heads slightly downward as though inspecting the bottom. I moved on, out from shore cover as I normally did, trying not to spook any bass that might still be in ambush positions. Finning slowly along, I was not able to locate the fish in their normal cover. I began to notice more and more bass cruising about in the middle depth ranges—no deeper than 12 feet—most of them in that same downward-angled attitude.

There was a jungly hole with a canopy of tree branches that regularly held a large concentration of truly big bass. This morning it was empty. *Even the big ones?* I wondered. I found them shortly, not far from their normal supercover holding spots. They, too, were prowling in the head-down attitude. Not every bass I found that morning was on the move, but enough were to make it obvious that the cold snap had triggered some sort of response.

Since then, I have witnessed this phenomenon many other times. Bass seem to enter into a free-swimming state at the start of a frontal system. They're extremely active during this period, and they'll definitely feed. Both jump-type lures such as jigs, worms, or spoons and crank-type lures will cause strikes. It is an excellent opportunity to present a lure to the larger fish, which are normally holed up in extremely difficult postitions.

I also found that most of this free-swimming activity occurred during the early hours and in the late afternoon. It is the period immediately after the weather change that produces such activity—almost as though the bass have an understanding that conditions are going to develop that will force them into a less-active state.

As the weather trend continues, over two days, the bass do indeed slow their activity. I observed the big fish pushing farther back into their supercover mazes. Medium-size and smaller fish tended to melt back into cover that was near a break into deeper water. A weedbed that extended to a dropoff, for example, would be a favorite place. The fish didn't hold in the middle of the weeds as might be expected. Instead, they moved closer to the deep-water edge of the bed.

The bass were well into such locations at the end of three to four days of cold, bright high-pressure weather. It has sometimes been preached that light is the sole influence on the fish at this time, which is why they have descended or burrowed into cover so thoroughly. Other theories maintain that the high pressure that follows a front forces more oxygen into the water, thus allowing the bass to go deeper. Still other ideas suggest that changing pressure affects the swim bladder of the bass, causing them to slow down and go deep, or at the very least stop feeding. I cannot accept any of these theories as presenting the whole truth. The presence or absence of bright light is certainly one of many influential factors with which I will deal later on. If pressure works on fish at all the way it does on human divers, a bass need only to rise or drop several feet to be subjected to vastly changing pressure. That he is affected by small barometric changes is highly unlikely.

I've taken oxygen readings just before and several days after the passage of cold fronts, and I haven't found great variances in the middle depths, where many of the fish go. I did note both temperature and oxygen changes in the shallow water after the arrival of a frontal system of several days when the weather remained unsettled and there was some wind. The oxygen improved, the temperature dropped. I believe that there is some water mixing during the passage of a front—both from wind action and from the descent of air-cooled surface water. Surely this changed oxygen supply affects the metabolic rate of the fish to some degree, in the same manner that it does to a great degree in winter. I know that smaller lakes seem to respond faster to frontal systems than some larger water bodies, just as they do to overall seasonal changes. The smaller lakes, for instance, are often best to fish in spring because they begin to warm up earlier. But a sudden reversal to the cold of winter can kill the action in these little lakes as though somebody threw a switch.

So we have oxygen, temperature, and light that can contribute to a change in bass behavior in the days after a cold front. I think that as further study is done a connection will be established between the effect of weather trends on bass prey and the subsequent movements of bass. It is possible that much bass forage is driven from its usual shallow environment both by temperature changes and by the wave action typical of a frontal system.

As the days warm again, bass will revert to their normal routine. One trend will have ended and more typical weather for the season will occur. It is important to remember that if the cold trend never lasted more than a day or two, it is most likely that no unfavorable change in bass behavior ever occured. In fact, the only alteration in routine was most likely one of activity—that free-swimming behavior in which bass cruise and feed in open water. This is an exciting time, one when even the big fish, which by day were as active as drowned logs, will be on the move. It's a good time to be on the water.

Storms

Most bass anglers I know feel that the best fishing weather is an overcast day with maybe a very light drizzle thrown in. I'll agree that can be one of the finest times to pursue bigmouths, but what about during a real cloudburst? Or how about those periods just after a summer downpour when the water quiets down, the sun comes out hot again, and everything is steamy? These times can be extremely productive, too, and it will pay to become acquainted with the reasons why and the methods that take fish then.

First of all, there's often no difference in the minds of many fishermen betwen cold fronts and storms. I make the distinction only to show how bass may be affected by trends consisting of wind and colder temperature followed by high barometric pressure vs. storms involving precipitation but not necessarily followed by any great temperature change.

Riding out storms underwater is a fascinating experience. Bass can have several different responses to a storm, depending on how long it lasts, how intense it is, and what precedes it. On the good side is feeding activity that can mean excellent angling. On the bad side are times when the fish seem to shut off completely. Fortunately the black moments are fewer and usually coincide with periods when you don't want to be afloat anyway. Imagine the following typical situation and you'll see what I mean.

It is midafternoon in early summer. Until just a short time ago, the sun was shining brightly. Now the wind has changed direction, picking up slightly, and big storm clouds have moved in quickly. They march toward the lake just as you slip in your scuba mouthpiece and dip beneath the surface. The underwater world has grown suddenly darker since the morning dives. At first, seemingly nothing has changed. Then you begin to notice. Small groups of largemouths are cruising at an increased tempo near the shoreline. You sink slowly to a typical observation position and wait.

Now bass that have been tight in cover begin to emerge. Small forage fish that have been hovering quietly nearby dart away or move closer to the protection of weedbeds. The situation is much like the first morning you observed the bass after the onset of a cold snap. But now the fish don't move with their heads angled down. You look up at the silvery surface and see that the first drops of rain have begun to fall.

The rain falls evenly at first, causing a steady pocking on the surface, which now seems even darker than before. You fin along, watching. Even more largemouths are now to be seen trading near shore cover, moving along weedbeds that extend into mid-lake. Finally the big fish stick their heads out of the supercover, emerge, and swim away. You are again tempted to try following them, but the 3 -to-6-pounders are far more tolerant of your presence, and so you move and continue to watch them. A flash here and there at the edge of your vision tells you that some fish may be feeding. But it is becoming harder to breathe and you abruptly realize your partially filled air tank has run dry. Your partner is about out, too, and so you both return to the boat, where a third man waits with additional compressed-air cylinders. A quick change and you are ready to go again. But this time the man in the boat will go to work, too.

You watch from below as the boatman casts a fat type of plug alongside a great log that extends from shore. The lure parts through the surface commotion caused by raindrops, digs down maybe 5 feet, and starts its frantic shaking. It goes maybe 3 feet. Bang! You never even saw where the bass came from, but he has nailed the lure, gone up once through the surface, and is now fighting to get back to the heavy cover. The man in the boat catches several more fish, moving on slowly, then changes lures. He has a floater-diver on now, jerking it under, swimming it, then letting it dart back to the surface. You rise to let him know that it is no good. The pelting rain on the surface is making it nearly invisible. He next tries a surface plug, one with propellers that churn and bubble and can be seen despite the rain disturbance. He takes two more fish, and then the steady pocking rain changes into a torrent. The water surface goes from darkish to silvery again. You rise to see how things look from above. The water surface is literally smoking with hard rain.

Slowly, at first, then steadily so there is no doubt, the bass begin to curtail their activity. Some of them seem to drift deeper; others move far into cover. Many seem to disappear before you can see where it is they are headed.

The scene repeats itself time and again with little variation. Bass feed during the early period of a downpour. But if the storm continues for some time, they will slowly decrease their activity. I believe there are several factors responsible for the increased tempo during the early part of a storm.

Bass seem to become more active if the sky growns dark quickly before a storm. If a storm approaches slowly and the sky grows duller gradually, the fish don't become quite so active. I have seen this sequence work this way enough times to feel there is some correlation. If the sky darkens and a wind gently riffles the surface (which has previously been quite calm), bass normally become active even before the rain actually begins to fall. These are the good storms.

The storms that seem to bother bass on many occasions are *heavy* electrical disturbances. Such weather can start with a productive fishing period just before the storm hits unless there is much lightning and thunder. Distant electrical disturbance will not bother bass too much, but let such a storm come close with great jagged bolts of lightning and booming thunderclaps, and the fish will begin to turn off. They'll head slowly into cover or deeper water. If you are wise, you will curtail your boating activity and head in also.

Another type of short-duration storm can help your fishing. It is the sudden summer downpour that takes you by surprise. It may very well be accompanied by quick electrical fireworks, but it is always quite brief. It produces its best effect during a hot spell. Generally you run out of it if possible. But whether or not you have been forced to endure a drenching, you should fish immediately after such a storm when the sun comes quickly out and the ground and surrounding vegetation literally steam. Such sudden showers freshen more than the surrounding countryside. Bass can give explosive sport for a brief time following such precipitation.

Rain of longer duration can have a variety of effects. Some of them are good; others cause problems. One of the positive results (from the fish-catching standpoint) is stained water. The very force of rainfall can produce better fishing in ultra-clear water, but a muddy runoff that is the result of rain can actually produce a form of ambush cover for bass as long as it does not become too widespread. I have found bass scattered along the length of a stain line that extended straight out from shore. That they were using this "mud" for camouflage was doubly confirmed when the effects of wind and current bent the stain in a new direction. The bass followed.

Rains that last for days will produce the bad effects on bass fishing. For example, where once a distinct mud line extended into clear water, a large area will have become discolored. The water will be heavy with silt. If the rain keeps up, the water level will rise across the entire lake, changing the locational habits of the fish and forcing you to relearn an area you thought you knew.

One-day or two-day rains can help anglers, especially in hot weather, by carrying extra food into a lake. There are two ways in which this can happen:

• First, rain will swell feeder streams, causing them to yield all sorts of extra forage. Worms, nymphs, crayfish, and minnows will be swept either from the stream itself or from crumbling banks. Not all of this forage is directly consumed by bass. Certain insect life provides the mainstay for smaller fish, upon which bass feed. These smaller fish will be attracted to the mouth of a swollen stream, and the bass will follow them.

• The second way in which runoff carries food to bass is directly from the lake's own banks. It is easy to locate feeder streams whose mouths may become hot spots after a rain. But it's somewhat more difficult to find the paths of bank runoff, especially in dry weather. If you cruise a lake near shore, you'll see some of the little gullies that past runoff has caused in the sloping banks. If the banks have fairly sparse vegetation, such gullies may be quite noticeable. Where heavier cover grows, you'll have to search for them but they're worth prospecting for. Worms and other likely forage creatures are channeled into the lake from the gullies. The water around the point where bank runoff enters may be totally devoid of good holding cover. Without rain bass may shun it, but during a steady rain, the bigmouths often stack up in numbers. Not every runoff will be a bonanza, obviously, but you'll find some that make the search worthwhile.

Wind

Some fishermen believe that wind has little effect on fish behavior. You have already seen how the buildup of wind-caused currents can reposition bass and move them from normal holding structure. There are still other important ways that wind influences bass behavior. Mild breezes, for example, can often seem to throw a magic switch that starts bass feeding. I've seen it happen from above and below the surface. Underwater, though, it completely eluded me at first. A flat slick water surface was tickled by a breeze, and the ripply ceiling did something. It doesn't always work that way, but it works often enough for you to try exploiting the situation.

Stronger erratic wind that laps grassy shorelines and builds the water up into little peaks (which are then sent marching away in another direction) can also set bass into motion. I couldn't understand why this should happen, especially since it happened only with certain wind patterns. The answer finally became evident. With particular wind-triggered wave action, it was becoming mighty uncomfortable for various young fish and forage minnows in their weed-root nurseries. They were rocked and washed in and out by wave action. Some moved deeper while others milled about trying, it seemed, to achieve some sort of stability.

The bass understood something about easy pickings. They were there, and they grabbed the minnows that darted down looking for new cover. The bigmouths also made sudden forays close to shore for the younger fish that rocked and danced about. But once the bass completed their slashing runs, they moved out. Not into deep water, just out of the more severe wave action in the extreme shallows.

Wind also affects the vital factor of boat control. If you haven't learned to consider wind when positioning your boat, then your fishing success will undoubtedly suffer. Used correctly, wind can work in conjunction with an electric motor or one of those nylon sea anchors (sold by many outdoor-equipment mail-order houses) to improve your fishing. What you strive for at all times is controlled drift—a drift that has been slowed enough so that you can cast and retrieve and still achieve lure and line control. If you can't sense what the lure is doing, then you're not fishing effectively.

If I were asked to make one overall statement about localized weather trends, it would have to be this: bass become most active at the *start* of changes in conditions. They can be nervous, fast-moving, cautious, but so are other species then. And this behavior may only be because there is a sense of urgency—such as land animals often display before a cold front or storm—to feed and then seek shelter. Because fish are in an agitated state, it is better to work them from a greater distance, not right on top of them as you must when they are hidden in supercover. But the start of a stormy trend is a good time to be fishing. It's a time when predators are feeding.

Hot-Weather Environment

The earlier-mentioned summer doldrums is the time when bass develop a severe case of lockjaw and all smart fishermen sit in the shade sipping at a tall cool one, right? Wrong.

Hot weather can be tricky, but it's not impossible. Most anglers know that a bass's metabolism increases during the warm weather. So the fish must eat more. Many anglers say that you can't prove it by them. Well, it's true. Largemouths do consume more, but they do it in fast, gluttonous spurts. There's another thing: In summer, it's quite possible that the bass in your lake are confined to very limited areas because of reduced oxygen content in much of the water.

Logic tells you that in summer, bass would want to go deeper to escape intense sunlight, higher water temperature, and increased boat and water-skier traffic. The assumption is valid. But if there is not enough oxygen deeper, the bass just cannot descend. I've fished and dived in many lakes where the oxygen fell off drastically before you even reached the thermocline, where the water temperature begins to drop rapidly.

Bass do not necessarily remain in water with barely adequate oxygen levels just to be in the deepest water they can. If there is more oxygen to be found elsewhere, they are as likely to be in it whether the higher oxygen content be in the shallows or near some mid-depth holding structure. Or the bass might be in a free-roaming state. They'll remain surprising lengths of time in the shallows, even if the temperature is high, as long as they have good

Author makes oxygen and temperature tests along good bass-holding structure.

cover. More often you'll find them farther offshore, especially around the ends of long tapering points. They'll also frequently be over some structure that rises from the oxygen-barren depths. It depends on the lake and the individual bass themselves. You have to make a thorough search to find concentrations of bass in summer. In hot weather, many seemingly ideal locations—places like the flats that were so productive in spring—will be devoid of largemouths.

In natural lakes some of the better places to search for bass concentrations include those points I just mentioned. Especially good are points that run from shore, dip down, and then rise up to form an offshore island. Also good are points that run from an island to an underwater reef. The dips of contour between points are often called saddles. The bass hold at the low point of the saddle or slightly above it if oxygen is a problem. Slopes with plenty of rock rubble also attract bass in natural lakes. Another excellent summer bass location is weedbeds.

Weeds are a subject in themselves. You should learn the depths at which certain types of weeds grow in your lake, and which of them hold more fish. During extremely hot weather, you may expect bass to station themselves both deep within the weedbeds and also on the shoreside edges. They will position themselves quite high in calm weather, no doubt because of the security they feel from the umbrellalike branching weed growth. Deep in the weeds, bass will respond only to a lure that is presented at a precise angle. Truthfully, they may only be able to see a lure that is worked in a particular attitude. This is why it is so important to work a weedbed from many angles until you have covered all presentation possibilities.

In man-made lakes, one of the key areas on which to concentrate your search for hot-weather bass is along old creek beds that were inundated when the reservoir filled. All the other usual man-made structure should of course be worked, but the main thing is timing. Remember, summer bass feed violently for short periods. For the greatest success, you must be on the water when they are foraging. Early and late in the day are naturally key times, but the fish can turn on at odd periods in between.

When summer bass are in the shallows, they are shouldered up in cover. This holds true for shallows near shore or out around the ends of tapering points. Bass also tend to utilize any small depression near this cover. A depression of little more than one foot may hold bass while nearby cover, seemingly equal in every way, is barren.

Hot weather is also marked by much off-structure schooling activity. And as you saw earlier, wind and moving forage fish are two reasons for bass leaving structure to which they normally relate. I've found bass quite far from their normal holding areas, but they usually return. Bass that have been wildly schooling on the surface often sink on the spot when they have finished their meal. They may be in water 60 or more feet deep but actually suspended only 10 to 20 feet below the surface.

Offshore bass that are not actively feeding (yet are not in a negative state in which they refuse to bite), present another situation with which you'll have to deal in summer. Here's a trick that should help:

To take large fish from a school of bass suspended over an offshore hump or rise, try working a lipped diving-type lure abnormally slow. These lures normally get their depth by being cranked at a pretty good rate. So to bring them down and keep them down while slowly crawling them, you must add weight. One of the better ways to do this is to thread a cone sinker onto your line ahead of the lure. You can also use split shot or rubber-core sinkers 10 to 12 inches ahead of the plug. Retrieve the plug with its lip knocking bottom. This technique can do wonders on those offshore bass. There will come a time, however, when even the best tricks will have a hard time luring largemouths. This is why:

Though bass metabolism increases with water temperature, it does not do so indefinitely. There is a cutoff point beyond which feeding activity decreases. That point is approximately 80°F. When the water temperature reaches 86°F., bass behavior becomes survival-oriented. The fish seek out any seep springs or feeder streams entering the lake. Any cooler water with enough oxygen becomes a sanctuary in which the fish will hold until conditions ease. Normally we don't have to worry about temperature extremes, but it's worthwhile considering the extent of the bass's adaptability in the face of great temperature stress. A study by James Siler and James Clugston has some important findings for fishermen.

The research of the two scientists occurred in the reservoir of a nuclear power plant. Water temperature in this reservoir was so high that the bass had to confine themselves to spring-fed and stream-fed sanctuaries most of the time from late spring through early fall. The areas in which they were confined were 2 foot high bands of water with temperatures from 70° to 77°F. Surrounding water was measured at 86° to 93°F.

The biologists tracked the fish by observing signals from tiny temperature-sensing transmitters that had been implanted in each bass. Water flow from the plant played an important part in the largemouths' movements. One bass left the sanctuary when the water temperature, which had been 95°F. in a weak flow, dropped to 91°F. in a much stronger flow. The bass followed this underwater current. The temperature eventually dropped to 80°F. When the water temperature again rose to 95°F., the bass returned to his cooler-water sanctuary.

One group of bass under study found a spring-fed sanctuary in a shallow cove. Here they remained, ignoring bright sun and the fact that little cover existed. They lived in water less than 3 feet deep. No bass over 10½ inches was found living in water warmer than 95°F. Some of the smaller largemouths (from a little over 8, to 10½ inches) were frequently tracked in water as high as 99°F.. One youngster was recaptured from water reading 102°F.!

Though normal fishing is not marked by such extremes, it is important to realize the impact of cooling, well-oxygenated underwater currents in a lake. This moving water from feeder streams and springs can act as a natural route for bass movements, as did the flow of water from the power plant. Rain runoff can also cause moving underwater currents, which bass follow after periods of extreme heat. Such currents can encourage largemouths to enter areas they previously avoided because of extremely high temperatures, low oxygen levels, or a combination of both.

In the Siler-Clugston studies, bass followed a layer of runoff water flowing along the bottom from heavy rain. Deadly temperatures hovered around them. When the rain ceased, the life-sustaining runoff trickled to a halt. Too far from their sanctuaries, the bass died. Though it's very unlikely that a cessation of rain runoff could kill fish in most of your fishing situations, it is well to remember how bass do rely on such currents.

Another summer situation seems in conflict with some things fishermen have learned about bass. It also gives substance to the belief that dog-day bass just don't bite. Let's say you have an area of good weedbeds running not far from a nice point that extends from shore. The bed produced well all during early summer, though the water was a mite too clear, you suspected, for the kind of sport you thought the place could produce. But lately the water has seemed to cloud up. In fact quite recently it has become downright murky. Good color, you thought. Ought to make every bigmouth in the neighborhood confident, and feeding well, too. But the fishing dropped off unbelievably. What happened?

The problem is a common one in most fertile lakes. It is caused by the buildup of tiny, free-floating plant organisms called algae during extended periods of hot weather. The algae plants color the water slightly and help provide some shelter from bright sunlight. Algae also give off oxygen during the day in the process known as photosynthesis, which every high-school student learns about in biology class. In the heart of summer, however, algae can build up to such an extent that sunlight may not penetrate the mantle more than a few inches. Without benefit of the sun, the deeper algae begin to die. Larger types of plants, rooted to the bottom, also become sun-starved and may die. Dying and rotting, the vegetation uses up oxygen in a process known as photosynthetic reversal. Such a condition can greatly reduce the oxygen in an area, causing bass to completely shun the place.

Borderline areas, those subjected to limited photosynthetic reversal, can hold fish in the afternoons after the sun has worked on them, but are poor in the mornings, after the darkness of night. Windless, cloudy weather makes this condition worse, but the mixing action of waves can relieve it somewhat. For avoiding areas hit by reversal problems, an oxygen meter really earns its keep in summer.

Cold-Weather Environment

The first series of observations I made underwater on Northern largemouths in cooling water seemed to refute all that I had learned about Southern largemouths in cold weather. It took a little while before the obvious dawned. These observations were being conducted in a small, shallow, natural, weedy lake, which can be the most difficult kind of lake for bass anglers once cold weather sets in. It doesn't matter where such a lake is. Bass respond far quicker to the seasonal change in such shallow-water bodies.

With the onset of cold, there is no gradual relocation of the fish from summer haunts to winter structure. The bass move out from the shallow cover and hole up in the deepest water they can find. Try to imagine what it's like for a largemouth to winter over in a lake whose deepest water is 20 feet in a climate where the winter temperature drops to minus 25°F. It's a marginal existence at best.

Wherever you find open water, there's hope for bass fishing. Here Dr. Mark Canter of New Jersey shows good bassing form despite bulky snowmobile suit, boots, and winter gloves.

When cold snaps hit the South, the smaller lakes are affected first. The bass can react so quickly that many largemouth anglers are led to believe that winter bass just don't bite. You go over into a deeper lake, though, and you've got an entirely different story.

Deeper lakes have a definite transition period after lake turnover (discussed earlier under seasonal behavior). The bass begin shifting from the long, gradually sloping points and inshore supercover to the steeper shores. Some bass simply move out from their summer holding places and suspend themselves at various depths, depending on local weather trends. Offshore structure is favored to a great degree by bass in cold weather. If the lake has no real terrain irregularities, largemouths will drop down into low bottom vegetation that, unlike the taller weeds of summer, does not die in cold weather.

Another area where I've found bass congregating in cold weather is off stone riprap at a dam or around dam-control buildings—especially if they're situated out on cement pilings. On fair, unseasonably mild winter days, bass often rise toward the surface as fishermen for years have said they do. It may be that the fish rise to absorb the rare weak rays of sun on those mild days, but I cannot say for certain.

In the ultra-clear desert-canyon lakes of the West, largemouths may descend extremely deep during the first late-fall cold snap—50 to 80 feet is not unusual.

In lakes with much varied terrain, largemouths locate along the steeper sides of underwater humps and also along the channels of any creeks that existed before the reservoir was constructed. If any timber still stands along such old creek beds, things will be even better. Bass tend to school near such timber. Their movements tend to consist in vertical repositioning rather than the horizontal free roaming they do other times of year.

Where shad are a primary forage species, bass take advantage of the first cold-weather kill of these baitfish. The little shad flutter down, flashing silver as they die. The bass wait below for a last feast before winter moves in solidly. During and following this period throughout the cold weather, an extremely successful method for catching bass is vertically jigging with spoons or a variety of leadhead jigs. The vertical jigging seems to duplicate the fluttering action of the dying baitfish. Still, largemouth metabolism is slow during cold weather. The fish don't eat as regularly as they do in warmer weather. In fact, biologists have shown that bass in cold water may feed as seldom as once every two weeks. And when they do, they certainly do not gorge. A single minnow may suffice.

How can a fisherman expect any success against such odds? The answer is that bass will strike in cold water, though it may be just a reflexive action. The bass school quite tightly in cold water. Generally they stack up along desirable structure. The exceptions are those periods when they are hugging the low-growing weeds. A persistent angler can take bass in cold weather by working the vertical jig along those creek channels I mentioned, or near riprap, pilings, steep shorelines, or standing timber.

The biggest problem in cold weather is finding the fish. To say they are concentrated is an understement. When I first started an underwater search for cold-water bass, I simply had too much territory to cover for the brief periods I was able to endure the water. Even with a good wet suit, gloves, and hood, I found it difficult to take 40 degree temperatures too long. Finally I had to run compass bearings back and forth in a search plan until I found the fish.

Anglers who've searched for the bass schools by boat while vertical-jigging know how tough it can be. You can jig all day along standing dead trees until you're muttering to yourself in frustration. Then, just before quitting time you may find the magic tree. Truthfully, there may be only one tree in a large area that is holding bass. If you get a vertical jigging spoon in front of these fish, the action can be fantastic. But if you cast a normal plug and bring it past them, you might not get a strike.

The fish just will not run down and capture a lure during cold weather. I've proved this over again many times by working with an above water fishing partner while I went below. I had plugs, spinners—just about everything—cast and brought past the suspended school. At least some fish in the school would regularly turn and watch the lures pass by. Sometimes one or two bass would actually seem to move slightly toward the lure. But they never got very far. There was no longer any doubt. The stacked schools absolutely refused to chase a lure. The jigging spoons were another story.

I found two main reactions of the fish to the vertically jigged lures.

· Sometimes they would allow a spoon to flutter and dance nearby for quite some time before taking it. They would move quite close to a lure jigging at their level. Then when they attacked they would surge forward even further, flare their gills in the usual manner, and take the lure. Every bass I saw take a spoon did so as the lure dropped. This is the most difficult time for an angler to detect a take, and the only thing for it is concentration and continued practice.

· The other way in which largemouths took a vertically jigged spoon was also on the drop, but when the lure was above them. When you jig an area without knowing exactly where the fish are holding, you either start from the bottom and work up, or you start from the top and work down. The bass that moved to take a dropping spoon worked above them would invariably angle their heads upward, rise, and then wait for the spoon to flutter down toward them. I saw no bass descend to take a spoon, but there may be conditions under which they will.

My observations were made near standing timber and along the branches of large trees that had fallen out into the water. The upper branches now reached out close to the first bottom dropoff into deeper water.

Another method I've seen work well on cold-water largemouths is best used along steep banks or stairstep rock ledges. It involves the use of ultra-light jigs and straight-shaft spinners of the type normally used for trout. These lures are in the ⅛-to-¼-ounce class. This is horizontal fishing for bass that are not suspended too deeply. You need calm weather so that the light line you must use will not be buoyed up by wind. This fishing entails casting out in the normal way and letting the light lures settle. The reason it works is that such light lures literally float by the bass. The lures hang long enough in front of the fish for even sluggish largemouths to have time to respond. I've found the best way to make this method work is to do very little reeling.

You should position yourself, cast, and let the lure settle until it hits one of these ledges. Next, give the lure an easy hop, pull it toward you with the rod tip, and then immediately lower the rod so that the lure will continue falling close to whatever structure you're working. If you don't lower the rod, your lure will swing out from the structure; the fish certainly will not move to follow it.

You can use this method for prospecting along banks or other promising areas by casting out not too far, following through with the settle, then extending each subsequent cast until you reach your cast-distance limit. Then move your boat to the point where your lure entered on the farthest cast, and begin again if the section farther on looks promising.

Having watched the fish too long for my own good in cold water, I cannot emphasize too strongly your need to concentrate on each subtle line movement. If you hit one fish, keep working the area. You can be pretty sure that other bass are close at hand. That's not always true in warm weather, but frigid-weather largemouths seem to like close company. Even if a sudden storm starts dumping snow over the water, don't head in right away. For some reason, the bass sometimes seem to get almost as excited during a heavy snowfall as they do during the early period of a rainstorm in mild weather.

3

How Light And Color Affect Bass

How Bass See

The light-blue-and-silver balsa plug sailed through the sunlight and landed with a gentle splat. It was off-target, possibly 5 feet out from the peak of a rocky spire formation that barely broke the still water surface. It didn't matter that the cast was short.

Before the lure could be moved, really almost before it hit the water, the slender plug was socked from below. The bass came up and went over in one splashy movement. The line tightened, the hooks went in, and the fish boomed for deep water—just for an instant. Then he came up all the way. He cleared the water, gills splayed, head shaking, mouth open wide.

The next run was toward shore and the knot of weed growth that filled a little cove. It was a good fight. And when it was finally over, the largemouth was slipped gently back to swim away. I wished I had been taking motion pictures from beneath the surface instead of still shots from the boat.

From beneath the water surface, largemouth bass have the ability to see the approach of potential food or danger. If it is a probable meal sailing through the air, a bass can easily move into position to intercept it. Consider this: I know of a gentleman who keeps a pond stocked with largemouths that he has conditioned to expect food at the sight of a human on the pond banks. The bass jump vertically clear of the water to snap food from an outstretched hand. Beyond that, if a morsel of food is tossed high into the air, the bass will see it dropping toward the surface and rush to grab it when it hits, sometimes before it lands. They are able to do this only on calm days when the water surface is not disturbed by wind or rain, but still the ability indicates the excellent vision possessed by bass.

Complete individual control of each eye (it's called monocular vision) enables bass to see what is happening on all sides except for a blind spot directly behind. The left eye of bass at right is getting the best look at the photographer. The right eye has begun to pivot in another direction.

The underwater vision of bass has some special features that adapt the fish for life as basically an ambush predator. For example, the curved shape of the bass's eye lens allows 5 times more light to enter the fish's eye than enters a human's eye. This lens shape also gives more peripheral vision. Conflicting reports have insisted the bass is farsighted and nearsighted. Nearsighted is

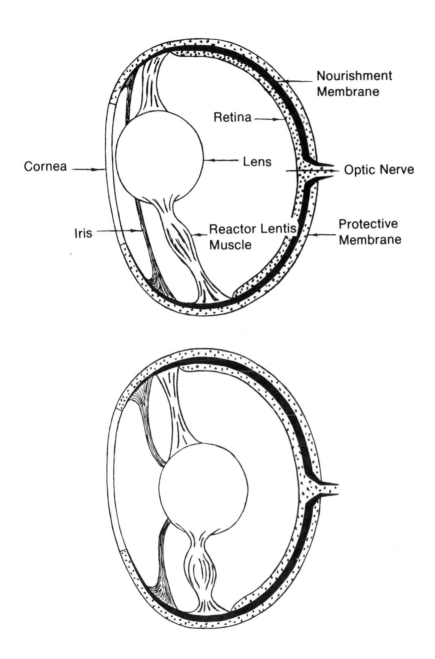

Top: Bass eye showing parts. The eye in this illustration is in relaxed condition, focused mainly on near objects. Above: Bass eye in the distance-focused condition. Note, too, that in this position the lens is farther from the cornea and that the lens does not protrude as far past the iris. Less light, therefore, enters the eye in this distance-focused condition.

closer to correct, but that description does not give the total picture.

In the relaxed position, a bass's eye is focused for near objects, but the fish does have the ability to focus on distant objects, too. Extreme distance focusing ability is not important to the fish. Even in the very clearest water, visibility is limited compared to air visibility.

The human eye focuses by flattening its lens. A bass's eye focuses on distant objects when the *retractor lentis* muscle pulls the lens back toward the rear of the eye. When the lens is pulled back like this, less light falls upon it. The effect is much the same as a person squinting to see a distant object clearly.

The subject of light entering the bass's eye has been one of debate. Because a bass's eye is not equipped with a pupil that contracts in the presence of light, and because a bass's eye has no lid, people have assumed that the fish cannot stand bright light. This assumption is not true on several counts.

First of all, even on bright days the light from the sun is subdued underwater. Second, the eye of a bass controls the amount of light affecting it through the type of receptor cells in use at the time. Third, regardless of all scientific reasons, it is a fact that station-holding as well as moving bass can often be found in the brighter underwater areas rather than shade.

The receptors in the eye of a bass deserve a little discussion. An understanding of the way they operate will help your fishing. The receptors in the retina of a bass's eye are in the form of rods and cones. Which type is used depends on the light level.

The cone cells go into use when the light level rises in the morning. They are also the color receptors. Toward evening, or when the light level is reduced because of weather or depth, the rods come into use. The rods are about 30 times as sensitive as the cones, but they are not color receptors. When they are in use, a bass sees in shades of gray, black, or white.

The rod cells, when not in use, move back into dark pigments in the retina of the bass's eye. Here there is protection for them from bright light. As light decreases, the rods move forward and the cone receptors move back where the rods had been. This changeover from rod to cone receptors is not instantaneous.

Normally it begins to occur near sunset. (A predator like the bass adjusts to light changes more quickly than many of the forage fish on which it feeds.)

The reverse adjustment normally happens near dawn. A bass begins switching over from night to day vision just before dawn. If you've been fishing all night and experience a lull when the first grayness of false dawn appears, wait. Because of its excellent light-adjustment abilities, a bass will be ready to attack its prey by daybreak, a time when the forage fish have not quite finished their switch to daylight vision.

During the period that fish have their night vision, they can be shocked in shallow water by bright light suddenly flashed in their eyes. The bass is no exception. Fish develop a sensitive bio-rhythmic "clock" within themselves. If it is upset, they will cease feeding. Such clocks can, however, develop a cycle around artificial stimuli. For example, bass can time themselves to take advantage of dock or boathouse lights. They lurk on the dark side of the shadow line while forage fish swim into the light to feed on plankton or insects. When the forage fish stray over the line of shadow, the bass nab them. If such lights are on during regular evening hours, the bass will nicely adjust themselves to the pattern. But if you turn these lights on irregularly, you will most likely spook any bass present.

Because of these physical visual capabilities, it seems safe to say that we can do away with another long-held myth: Light does not bother bass just because they don't have eyelids or contracting pupils as do humans. This is not to say that light does not affect bass behavior. We've already discussed how artificial light can positively or negatively affect largemouths. We've seen how bass take advantage of the changeover period from day to night vision (and vice versa) to ambush prey that had slower visual adjusting ability. Now consider some other reasons that light affects largemouths.

As fingerlings pursued by many different kinds of larger predators, bass quickly learned the relationship between heavy cover and safety. Thick cover also screens out light. Surely a connection must become imprinted upon the young bass: *Dim light means safety.* As I observed more and more schools of fingerlings underwater, I became convinced that the assumption is correct. Out of heavy cover, the young bass consistently hover in the shadows of natural and manmade structure. The abutments of bridges, piers, a single boulder, or a large fallen tree trunk are good examples. What about fishable-size bass?

As largemouths grow older, they learn to use the cover of reduced light for ambushing during other than the rod-cone vision turnover periods. Bass take advantage of reduced light both in the shallows and in deeper water, where they frequently lurk below forage species in the dimness. Older bass also remember the lessons of youth. Though as adults they have far fewer enemies, bass still display their liking for reduced light when frightened.

I performed a series of experiments that proved this point to my satisfaction. I worked on groups of bass that were located out of heavy cover in the shallows, others that were near various forms of shallow to mid-depth structure such as pilings or rock outcroppings, and those fish that were holding off-cover near some structure in open water. I made these tests in very clear water so I could get some distance from the fish and still see them without disturbing them whatsoever. Still, as in all my observations, I waited awhile so that the only movement was from my bubbles, which I tried to keep as quiet as possible by slow, gentle breathing.

Above, a friend in a boat would wait the time we had agreed upon. Then he'd move in on the fish that I had pinpointed for him. He would alert the fish by various means, coming directly over them with the boat and stopping, then doing things like scraping a tackle box or knocking against the boat with a hard object, churning a paddle in the water, or causing a shadow to hover over the bass.

Depending on how badly the bass were spooked, they had a variety of reactions. Severely frightened bass would simply scoot off for deep water. Nervous fish would inevitably move to the shadowy side of any structure or cover that existed in the area. The open-water fish would just drop deeper or toward the darker side of any hump or sunken island nearby. Fish that were a little more frightened would try to get as close to the cover or structure as possible, but always on the shady side or section.

I am left with the conviction that low light levels mean security to bass of all ages and that low light also means good ambush country for fishable-size largemouths. Light level is, of course, directly dependent on the nature of the water, and on the prevailing weather.

The weather-water correlation is why bass anglers fish by the following game plan:

• *Colored water,* work the shallows.

• *Clear water,* fish deep unless it's raining, foggy, or overcast.

The formula is successful to a large degree, but as we've seen in an earlier section, you can also find bass deep in colored water or shallow in clear water even in fair weather. The largest bass can be reluctant to bite in the shallows during bright weather, however. Medium-size bass or yearlings still provide excellent sport under such conditions.

Though the sun is never as bright underwater as above, light penetration in the shallows at midday, is considerable in the clearest of lakes on a crystal day. Using an underwater photo exposure meter, I watched the rapid drop of light that occurred as the sun's angle to the earth decreased. Water acts as an excellent reflecting medium, greatly cutting down the penetration of the sun's rays except at high noon.

If you keep these factors in mind, watching the movement of shadows as they relate to other known cover, you should increase your bass-fishing success. Just don't fall into the trap of thinking that largemouths are always stuck in the shade. There is usually cover near if bass are in the shallows, but that cover is often quite sparse and unable to reduce the light levels effectively. I've frequently located groups of bass tight to bare tree branches right next to shore, or in branches of standing timber on humps away from shore. The sun was out, and the bass were not in shadow. Deeper water close at hand was a handy route to the safety of dimness and depth. Nevertheless, the bass were holding shallow out of shade in bright weather.

In addition, roaming bass pay little attention to bright light and are as likely to be moving near the surface inshore as they are in open water. Bass that are following schools of forage fish will do so in open water away from any shade-making cover. If they choose to remain out of sight, they do so by descending. That is the only way such bass can lower the existing light level in which they are operating.

When Vision Counts Less

Earlier we saw that though bass are able to focus on distant objects, they're primarily concerned with what happens within that magic 15-foot radius of awareness in all directions from them. But bass cannot always see even 15 feet. Visibility in many lakes is limited to a few feet, in some cases a few inches. Still, the fish are aware of what happens nearby. At night or in dingy water, bass rely on other sensory abilities. They're fully able to detect odors in the water. Their ability to sense vibrations as a combination of sound and touch will be covered in another section, but it's important to make a comparison here between that ability and vision.

Bass, like other biologically successful animals, have the ability—within certain extremes—to adapt to their environment. Many country people often wonder how city people survive the frantic pace of urban living, yet they find themselves adjusting quite well if they later take a job in a large metropolitan area. I have never been able to handle that specific adaptation, but many people are quite successful at it. Now if you take a bass from extremely clear water and put him in dingy water, he will have trouble at first. The trouble will arise from the fact that he has developed his visual abilities greatly while his other sensory capabilites have not had to do much work. The result is that he will not be able to catch his food as well as the bass who has always lived in murky water.

Documentary film producer Glen Lau discovered just how great an impairment such environmental switching can be to largemouths. Lau keeps various fish species in huge aquariums for study. He generally keeps these tanks dark to retard the growth of algae. In one aquarium, Glen had a group of largemouths that had originally come from a murky lake. At one point he added some additional bass that had come from a particularly clear-water environment. Also in the tank were shiners and other forage fish.

The next time Glen looked into the tank after adding the clear-water bass, he was amazed. The original largemouths were fat and healthy. The newcomers had battered and bloody noses and were slimmer around the waistline. The clear-water bass, accustomed to feeding by sight, had butted their front ends into the glass tank while trying to capture the shiners. The dingy-water bass had never had such a problem, for they homed in on their prey by using senses other than sight. Because the clear-water bass were smaller, Lau was able to distinguish them from his original fish. To make certain of his findings, he performed the experiment again, keeping clear-water and dingy-water bass in separate tanks. The results were the same.

Doesn't this suggest something that has direct application to your fishing? If clear-water bass rely that heavily on their visual acuity, you'd better make sure your tackle is as close to perfect as possible. Such critical bass call for light-weight lines, small lures, and precise presentation with lures rigged to run properly.

Other Senses

It's difficult to separate three of the bass's faculties: (1) his ability to taste, (2) his ability to detect odors, and (3) his ability to discriminate through feel an object taken into his mouth. As with humans, all these sensory capabilities most likely work together. If, for instance, you should take a mouthful of spoiled food, your sensing capabilities work together to let you know that you've chomped down upon something bad. If a bass can leisurely inspect, then take a bait and one of his senses tells him something is wrong, he will reject the bait. However, there are times when one or more of the sensory receptors may be overriden.

Some anglers have wished to demonstrate the lack of importance of odors when bass fishing. To do so, they soaked their lures in one obnoxious solution or other. The bass still attacked the lures. However, the lures were fast-moving. Spoiling the odor of a slow-moving natural bait will frequently destroy its fish-catching ability. In the case of the lures that were exposed to repellent substances, the bass were responding to attractive vibrations plus what they saw, and they didn't stop long enough to get a good whiff of what they were biting.

Bass can detect the odor of extremely small quantities of various substances in water. There is one substance of great interest to anglers. It has been called the alarm substance. As this book goes to press, no studies by qualified biologists have been performed to show the workings of this substance on bass. But such work has been done on minnows *(Cyprinidae family)*. And several amateur naturalists have done such work and proven to their satisfaction that bass do emit the alarm substance when injured. Here's what has been discovered:

If a school bass is fairly hooked and then carefully taken from the water, dehooked, and released, he will return to the school with no reaction on their part except for closing ranks around him. But if that same bass is returned to the school with a break in its skin, the school's reaction seems to be quite different. The amateur naturalists who have performed the experiment report that as the injured fish heads for the school, the other fish will move away, opening a path in their ranks. They want no part of this injured comrade, who after a few minutes will usually give up trying to rejoin them and will head for cover.

The belief is that some sort of critical substance exists just beneath the skin of bass. A bass need not bleed to give it off. Evidence indicates that just a small break in the skin seems to release the danger odor. Yet natural lesion on the bass's skin does not seem to trigger the release of the scent. I have not personally tried this experiment, but fishermen should be aware of the possibility that such a warning odor exists.

Night Fishing

The sun had set and my underwater surroundings were rapidly growing too dark for me to see much, even in the clear water of the big sinkhole. I swam somewhat wearily back toward shore, making it a point to pass a bankside jungle of fallen trees that formed the supercover hangout of a group of extremely large bass.

I tried to check on these fish periodically during the day, because they never seemed to move from this shallow-water sanctuary, no matter what the weather did. Only once, at the start of a heavy rainstorm, did they break their school and begin roaming. When they were on station, I had occasionally been able to lure some of the fish from the group with the angling tactics described in the section on fishing supercover. I liked to watch these bass because they represented the real survivors among their species, and because they were just so big and impressive.

Now, in the growing dusk, I rounded the point where their log maze thrusts out from shore. I stopped, then let myself slowly sink without another motion. Something was happening. Several of the patiarchs of the group had turned from their usual positions. Their bodies rocked tail to nose. They flared their gills, opened and closed their jaws, and finned actively. It was the same "wake-up" movements that I had observed in smaller bass prior to a feeding session. I waited.

Several more of the big bass repeated the movements, then swam from the sanctuary and headed down and out toward open water. Soon another bass followed. Shortly, only two of the original 12 were left.

It was now far too dark, and I headed in with my thoughts on the breakup of the big bass group. On several other evenings I observed the same thing. I attempted to follow the fish, but they seemed bent on moving. I couldn't keep pace with them. Once on a night dive, I thought I might have located one of the group's big bass, holding near the bottom over the weeds at a place where a long point projected from shore. My light was an unnatural element, however, so except during spawning season, night observation underwater never showed natural behavior. Still, I did learn several important facts before continuing my observations abovewater.

First was a matter of vision. Without a light, I was virtually blind underwater at night. If it was a bright night or if I was swimming just at dusk, I learned it was easy to keep track of the silhouette of the dive boat that followed me. It was a white-hulled boat, but the bottom of it looked dark in the dim light. Eventually I began to relate the sight to angling for bass. Why else, I wondered, would surface lures that were scorned by bass at midday in clear water become so effective at night? Why else the choice of dark lure colors at night by long-time fishermen? Here was old-time bass lore that was accurate. The clearly visible silhouette of a surface plug on a bright night must be the reason that every fleeting glimpse I had of a bass at dusk showed the fish to be near the bottom in relatively shallow water. It was obviously the place for them to be in order to gain a better visual picture of potential forage swimming by.

It wasn't the whole story, of course. Bass obviously make use of the previously discussed sensory abilities during night feeding. Despite their ability to see better than human beings under low light levels, I am certain that without the use of their other sensory equipment they would not be able after dark to locate and attack a plastic worm swimming low in the water or a subsurface plug or spoon skimming the deep edge of a weedbed.

Bass, as any night fisherman can confirm, are not constantly active at night. While diving without a light at dusk, I came upon bass that were to my way of thinking sleeping. Perhaps that is not scientifically correct. But if they were not actually asleep in the way we think of sleep, they were certainly at rest. I found fish in this condition in several lakes and quarries in different parts of the country. They were on ledges or the bottom near various forms of weed growth. They rested in a normal swimming attitude, but their tails were slightly elevated. They seemed to be balancing on their fins, which were erect. I found fish in an inclined position both on a horizontal bottom and on steeply sloping banks or cliff walls. While using a light I also found "sleeping" bass at various times of night. In those cases, however, it was most likely the shock of light on their night vision that held the fish immobile as though they were asleep. When I consciously began looking for this sleeping behavior I observed it by day, also. The bass rested on their fins on the bottom and, except for very slight gill movements, were quiet.

From all this experience, I decided it would be tough to predict just when bass would feed at night. They could sleep or rest at any time. There was some correlation with bad weather, the fish beginning to feed much later at night, if at all, after a lengthy storm. I was left with the conviction that a bass fisherman had better plan to stick with his fishing all night if he hoped to be successful. I also decided that the color or finish of a plug did not

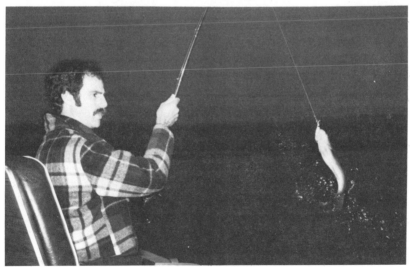

Night fishing, especially in warm weather, is an excellent way to catch some bass. Boat houses and docks (top) that held no bass by day frequently produce well at night because the fish move in from deeper water. Dr. Mark Canter (above) heaves in a battling largemouth, his reward for patient efforts.

matter much at night, but I found myself seeming to favor the darker colors. Line size, too, seemed to make little difference after dark, unless it affected the action of a delicately tuned plug. If you're happier using heavy line after dark, by all means use it.

Night fishing also seemed an answer to the problem of how to reach the largest bass in a clear-water lake if you wanted to avoid the supercover route. Time after time at dusk I saw the biggest bass leaving their holes or disbanding their stack-up formations. I figured that besides the safety factor that came with darkness, the smaller lakes tended to cool off a little on some summer nights. Though in warm weather bass generally feed more, the temperatures of some smaller ponds in the South climb so high that the fish feeding decreases or stops. Actual thermometer tests proved this was true, but it took a while to happen and the cooling was really most noticeable just before dawn.

Because larger fish were on the prowl at night, I chose to use big plugs. I could catch smaller bass by day, but the big fellows weren't that simple. Why not specialize in them by night? The theory, held as fact by anglers who have fished for bass at night far longer than I have, worked well for me. I also learned something about control.

I found myself missing far too many surface-feeding bass at night by striking at a splash. I learned how to wait before striking and to keep out slack that you can't really see building up after dark. I also learned the value of a consistent retrieve.

I believe that when there is no moon, bass have a tough time seeing the silhouette of a surface lure even with their better-than-human night vision. I think they home in on a lure by using their other senses to a large degree. I found that whether you use a stop-and-go retrieve or a steady swim, you should maintain the pace. I think bass fix on the rhythm of a retrieve. If it becomes erratic, they can overshoot or undershoot their mark. At least this is the only way I can explain those heavy swirls around of my surface lures that failed to result in solid strikes, even after I had learned to control my reflexes and hit only when I felt a fish solidly.

Moon Phases

I tried to establish some patterns between fishing success and phases of the moon. The only thing that seemed fairly consistent was that spawning activity frequently intensified with the approach of a full moon. But not always. Localized weather conditions punched holes in many of my theories. If weather was stable and the bass were ready, pre-spawning activity intensified during the four-day period prior to the night of the full moon. During this period, the fish would bite. If a rising water temperature coincided with this four-day period, you could really expect fantastic fishing success. Ideally the water temperature should be in the 50's and rising. With the actual full moon, the bass would normally spawn; fishing would drop off drastically for the next few days.

If severe cold weather occurred just prior to the full moon, the bass would hold off spawning until the full moon of the following month. When conditions finally permit a spawn to bass that have held off for a month or two, the period before the actual full moon can be truly wild for angling.

Various fishermen have different ideas about when the better night angling occurs. Some like a moonless night—even with a little rain. Others swear by a bright full or nearly full moon. Brackish-water bass are affected by the moon, which, of course, is related to the tides. It seems that many devoted night-fishermen take their largest bass in the dark of the moon. During periods without a moon, I've found that other bass seem to become disturbed with the commotion of a surface-fighting brother largemouth. After I catch one fish that puts up a good surface fight during a dark night, I usually can't take another fish from the immediate area for some time. During the full-moon periods, this problem does not seem to exist. But maybe the explanation is just that I'm more effective with a moon.

I personally prefer to fish during a moonlit night because I can see better and handle my tackle better. If you become extremely familiar with a lake (which you should, to be an effective night fisherman), you'll have little trouble on a dark night finding the areas that produce the better fishing. You may even find you'll take bigger fish then. But you won't get to see the silhouette of a mighty bigmouth thrashing at the edge of the weedbed in the silvery light from a buttermilk moon. And that, to me, is what really makes night fishing.

Color Preference

The largemouth bass may see color better than any fresh-water fish. Of course we don't know whether bass see colors just as we do, but considerable evidence indicates that bass do distinguish between various hues and actually seem to prefer some colors over others. *Prefer* may not be exactly the right word. It's possible that bass are just more sensitive to different colors, or that some shades just make them excited. Experimental psychologist Donald F. McCoy of the University of Kentucky is a pioneer in studying bass behavior. McCoy's choice of subject is no doubt influenced by the fact that in leisure hours he is an avid bass fisherman. I have been lucky enough to share in some of his studies, one of the latest concerning how color affects bass behavior.

Don McCoy established without a doubt that bass distinguish between various colors. In fact, he found that they can distinguish between shades of green that are not always discernible to the human eye. In his experiments, Dr. McCoy eliminated the possibility that the bass were responding merely to the brightness or intensity of color. To do this he used a complex filter system that we need not go into.

McCoy's bass were trained to attack a colored target to receive a food reward. One interesting sidelight was that once the fish learned that a particular color would result in food, they could not unlearn the fact. It follows then that a bass may learn something at any stage of its life and continue indefinitely the behavior that results from that learning.

From his work Don observed some fascinating behavior based on color preference. He conditioned some bass to expect a food reward for hitting a red, yellow, or green target. The bass responded equally to these colors. Next Don stopped rewarding the fish when they hit the target. The bass reacted by slowing their attack response to the target in this order: they still continued to respond well to the green target, somewhat slower to red, and slowest to yellow. McCoy began to believe that a preference for green existed.

Then it struck Don that his studies had not been done in an influence-free·environment, as he had wished. He realized the walls and ceilings of his laboratory were painted green. Of course the tank-held fish were subjected to the greenish overtones of the environment. McCoy then took some other bass and carried out the same experiment (with the target color blue added) in a colorless environment. The results were entirely different. After the food reward was taken away, the bass continued to respond best to red, then yellow, next green, and finally blue.

Did the new experiments invalidate the results of the first? "No," says McCoy. "What we are beginning to suspect is that color preference can be modified by the bass's environment."

This is a breakthrough for fishermen. If it continues to prove accurate, it may take the guesswork out of line-lure color selection. But there are factors to consider first. Though bass in a colorless en\ironment seem to prefer colors in the longer wavelengths (reds, orange, yellows), no bass lake I know has a colorless environment. Even what we refer to as clear water is tinted slightly. It is blue-green, bluish, reddish, the color of weak tea, or just plain muddy yellow or dark brownish.

In highly colored water, the color choice should be easy if you plan to try matching the environment as Dr. McCoy's research indicates you should:

· Dark opaque worms in dark water.
· Yellowish or chartreuse lures in lighter muddy water.

Clear water is trickier. The overall tint of clear water may not be discernible to you except underwater. Often, though, the surrounding lakeside vegetation or the underwater vegetation can give you a clue. Weather, too (a bright blue sky, for instance), will affect the tint. By experimenting, I found that the formula of matching lure finish to the tint of the water was proving pretty reliable. Then I hit a snag.

The problem arose in Utah's Lake Powell. As elsewhere, bass would take lures of various colors, but they were fairly consistent on red worms. At first I couldn't understand why. The water was extremely clear. The bright sky was a vivid blue dome. It took a while, but then I thought I had the answer. We were catching bass with plastic worms on crumbly rock ledges and rubble points. These structures were formed of rock that had come from the surrounding steep canyon walls. The walls of the canyon loomed up stark and red. Naturally that reddish overtone would permeate the clear water, even overpowering the effect of the sky close to the cliffs.

In the end, we must wonder whether bass are sensitive to wavelengths (colors) that are not even visible to man. The time will no doubt come when we will be able to learn such things. For now it is good that we are at least getting an inkling of the largemouth's preferences among colors we *can* see.

Every bass fisherman knows that in different places on different days, various colors are more successful than others. If you haven't proven that to yourself, you can do so by trying the same lure in a variety of finishes during a good bite (when the fish are feeding steadily.) Even during a schooling period when the fish are madly tearing into baitfish near the surface, one or two colors or finishes will usually prove more successful than others. Underwater, the results are even more startling.

My underwater observations proved that bass respond in a variety of ways to your lure colors, ways that you have no way of knowing about in a boat on the surface.

For instance there are negative responses to a lure: a bass can simply ignore the artificial or actually flee from it.

And there are a variety of what you would call positive responses. Fish can simply turn toward a passing lure and watch it. They can follow it for a ways inquisitively. They can chase a lure for some distance before breaking off the pursuit quite close to your boat. Or they can strike.

If I told you how many bass actively chase your lures without taking them, you wouldn't believe me at first. When I first told the anglers with whom I was working how many fish chased their plugs or spinners after I watched below, they thought I was giving them a big story. When they finally began to believe me, they became terribly frustrated. I try not to mention it any more.

Now I have another way to handle a color experiment. I ask two anglers to fish from the same boat. They use lures that are identical in every way except for finish. I can only make good observations of this experiment in clear water, so these tests have been limited to such water. I try to station myself inconspicuously while the anglers cast, switching rods or alternating which lure is cast first to a prime spot. The results have been fascinating.

The experiment has proven that different groups of fish definitely have particular color preferences on given days. Not all bass groups in the same lake will have the same preference on the same day, though that does sometimes occur. I also found that color preference is far less exacting the deeper the bass are.

Bass show a high degree of color discrimination with surface lures. There is also a high degree of color preference among slower-moving lures.

But bass seem to strike fast-moving lures more as a reflexive reaction. They have time for none of the leisurely examination of the lure that I mentioned earlier as one of the positive bass responses. Instead, largemouths respond quickly. They have to. Though lure color or finish may sometimes be responsible for a bass's turning away at the last moment, I'm convinced that with quickly moved lures it is action and general overall impression that triggers a strike response.

How Color Reacts

When you're considering a finish for slow-moving or surface lures, it is well to keep in mind something that scientists call positive or negative contrast. Will your lure look brighter than the surrounding background against which you swim it? How will light affect that lure? Anything that causes the lure to lose brightness or seem dark against a darkish background will cause it to be less visible.

A negative-contrast lure is one that will seem dark against a light background. Examples: (1) a dark lure on the surface at evening and (2) a lure that will be viewed horizontally in front of the light source.

After you've considered the backdrop against which your lure will be worked, you must think about what water does to color. Bass preference for a color at one depth is not a sign that the preference will hold true at other depths.

As you go deeper, colors lose their characteristics in varying degrees. Red, for instance, loses its characteristic first, turning brownish and finally black. Depending on the nature of the water, this change of appearance can happen in from 10 to 30 feet. Orange loses its characteristic next, followed by yellow, then green, and finally blue, which maintains itself to considerable depth.

Of course if you use red while fishing for bass in relatively shallow water, you needn't be concerned over how quickly that color can look like something else. Fluorescent dyes in paints and finishes react to daylight and to the ultraviolet rays that bombard the earth. Such fluorescent brighteners help colors to retain their characteristics far deeper underwater than do normal colors. For instance, I have personally seen a fluorescently brightened red maintain its characteristics to 27 feet. Other observers report that fluorescent reds and orange maintain their characteristics to depths of 45 feet.

Opaque colors seem to hold together solidly under most dim-light conditions. Translucent colors do something else. When struck by sun rays, they tend to pick up light and emit a glow. Depending on how the light hits them, they can develop a mottled appearance or remain fuzzy yet extremely visible.

Lures

We have considered the tint of the water, the background against which your lures will work, and how water itself changes nonfluorescent colors. How does the information apply to a fisherman's choice of lure finish?

I've reached the following conclusions, based on personal fishing and underwater observations:

• First, I haven't noticed any increase in bass-angling success by using fluorescent-finish lures in deeper water. It's true that the brightened colors maintain their characteristics to greater depth than do normal colors, but isn't it unnatural for bass to see these colors deeper? If so, the sight of a hot-orange plug scooting along at 30 feet or so may spook them. Other fish (salmon and lake trout for instance), seem pleased with the bright colors in deep water. But such finishes have not produced better deep-water bass catches or responses for me. In shallow water, however, especially if conditions are somewhat dingy, the fluorescents have been quite good. I especially like combinations of fluorescent colors arranged in patterns that simulate fish—yellow and green, for example.

• Aside from fluorescents, in water with poor visibility I find myself using solid or opaque-colored plastic worms—usually purple and black. For plugs and other lures, I like a metallic silver or gold finish; also white, lime green, chartreuse, or a combination of red and white.

In clearer water I'll inevitably choose translucent plastic worms. If the water has a brownish or reddish tint, I'll usually use red worms. When a clear sky prevails and I'm fishing clear water with limited vegetation, I'll usually use blue worms. I like to use this color for fishing around pilings, old cribbing and rocks. For plugs, I'll use white or bone or the metallic combination finishes: black back; silver, gold, blue, or green body; white belly. The crayfish finishes are also good.

Underwater I've noticed that bass sometimes show negative reactions to the metallic finishes. This usually occurs in clear water on very bright days. If everything else seems right and I've been fishing a flashy finish without catching fish, I'll suspect that it's just one of those days when the bass don't want such glitter. I'll change to either a natural forage-fish-scale finish or a red-and-white combination.

Line

There's a popular myth that as long as you can see your line well, its color is not important. This supposition may be true with many fish. Not with bass. On some days it's not so important; on others, the choice of line color and type is critical. We tend to fuss a great deal over the lures we use, especially their action and finish.

When it comes to line, many fishermen make a choice based on advertising claims, on what the local "pro" is using, or just on how pretty the line looks. No matter what we do, a line extending from a lure is still an unnatural-looking thing. By careful consideration of the water we're fishing and of the background against which our lures with line will be presented, we can make some decisions. Water depth, and background considered, the choice of line must be made on whether you want to disguise your line as much as possible, use it as an additional attractor, or incorporate it as a visual aid to your fishing.

Today we can choose clear, light-colored, dark-colored, and brightened lines. Your choice of line color must also be tempered with choice of line weight. The broadest statement I can make concerning line weight is that in clear water where your fishing will not be in the very thickest kind of timber or weeds, it is wise to use extremely light line. Do not, however, choose a line that's too light for you to cast a chosen lure with it.

I made a series of tests on line weight in clear water. I used strengths of line testing from 20 pounds down to 6. In every test, as the line test decreased, two things happened: (1) the number of hooked fish increased, and (2) the number of follows I saw from an underwater vantage point increased. When the sun was shining, the success of light line over heavy line increased even more.

Heavy line, besides having visual disadvantages, can affect the action of some sensitive or very light lures. The choice of light line must, or course, be evaluated against the number of fish you may lose on the lighter line. As previously mentioned, if you do not need to fish in the heaviest timber, you should not have much of a breakage problem. You must check a lighter line more frequently for fraying, and you can't horse bass around rocks and pilings without the heavier stuff. But other than those situations, there is no reason to fear using the light line. My personal choice is 8-pound-test, sometimes even 6-pound-test when I can use it. I do not like to use line heavier than 10-pound-test if I can possibly avoid it. In dingy water, the visual impact of line weight is considerably less important. Line color is the next consideration.

You'd think that the overall best choice would be a clear line because it is less visible to the fish. But it is not always less visible.

If we had a line that adjusted automtically to match the water clarity, we would have a nearly invisible line. We don't have such a line. Clear lines can look darker against a lighter background, or lighter against a dark background. Still they have low visibility underwater and are good choices for much all-around fishing. Dark lines, especially brownish-colored, are barely discernible when fished in front of mottled vegetation or brush. They are excellent for such subsurface fishing, but they tend to show up in silhouette when used on surface lures or against light backgrounds.

The lines that are brightened with various fluorescent dyes in the manufacturing process are another interesting matter. As a result of my spending many hours observing this line from fish level and seeing how bass react to it, I am left with some definite impressions:

· First of all, such brightened lines do not magically disappear from view underwater, especially in clear water. In fact, if you fish a slow-moving lure such as a plastic worm in the shallows in very clear water using a brightened line, you'll frequently reduce the number of fish you catch. Ultra-bright lines look bigger underwater, but they're not. This optical illusion is caused by the bright, glowing appearance of the line. In clear water, such glowing lines show up very well. This is not to say that bass will refuse all lures presented on bright lines in ultra-clear water.

· In clear water, the splashy entry of a lure will not necessarily disguise a brightened line. Depending on the angle of the sun, such lines can show up immediately. If you're fishing shallow water and the fish are spooky, this extreme line visibility can inhibit a strike. Depending on what background these lines are viewed against, they will show up well or tend to break up visually. The brightened lines that are more opaque tend to break up less than those that are more translucent. In general, blue or blue-green brightened lines tend to give the appearance of breaking up against a light bottom or multicolored vegetation (though they are still more visible than brown or clear lines). They also give this effect when viewed against the surface from below. Yellow-colored brightened lines are less visible against light or yellowish colored weeds.

· The angle of the sun does interesting things to the brightened lines. For instance, when viewed from underwater in clear to

Illumination has a lot to do with how a brightened monofilament line shows up underwater. Sometimes such a line affects bass negatively (usually in extremely clear water). If sun is directly at fisherman's back (top), line is very visible to fish. If sun is at fisherman's side (middle illustration), line gives appearance of breaking up to fish-eye view. If light is directly in fisherman's face (above), it will look bright to a bass if light falls in direction line is being retrieved.

marginally clear water the lines, if front lighted, show up extremely well. If they are backlighted, they show up well—but not quite as brightly as in a frontlighted situation. If these lines are sidelighted, they will appear far less bright; in the case of some lines, they will tend to break up in appearance.

• You do not need brightened lines when you're using crankbaits or for straight retrieves with surface lures or spinnerbaits. Where, then, do such lines fit in the angling picture? Experienced bass fishermen have learned that the best line is not always the most "invisible," especially in the colored or moderately dingy waters where most anglers fish for bass. Fishermen are finding that the ability to discern a slight twitch or "kick" of the line often makes the difference between catching or not catching bass. As plastic-worm specialist Bob Martin from Springfield, Missouri, says, "I watch that line all the time. I keep my eyes just glued on it. I concentrate so hard on the line I often get a headache."

This line-watching style of fishing is where the brightened lines really shine, if you'll pardon the pun. They're at their best in dingy water where the bass rely quite a bit on senses other than sight until the moment before they hit a lure. A plastic-worm fisherman or an angler who tightlines (keeps slack from developing in the line while the lure sinks) leadhead jigs, or flutters a tailspin or spinnerbait lure down to the bottom, owes it to himself to try the bright lines. Anglers who use natural bait and have their best results when they let a fish run a little way before striking, find the bright lines of help. Their trick is to watch the line carefully and open their spinning-reel bails or snap their casting reels into free-spool the moment the line starts marching off.

• The bright lines make it much easier to see the slightest twitch or line motion. When you have some concern about using bright lines because the water is especially clear, you can always try a technique used by generations of bass fishermen who never knew the benefit of monofilament. You can tie on a low-visibility leader that will be best suited to the conditions you must fish. Use a monofilament leader of from 5 to 15 feet. If you use a conventional casting reel, you may have some trouble getting the lineleader knot to pass through the level-wind bracket. If so, use a leader short enough to keep the knot outside this device. There will be no such problem when you're using a spinning reel. Normally a small neat knot like the Double Duncan loop or a blood knot will pass through the level wind and rod guides. If your rod guides are excessively small, I'd recommend replacing them with larger guides anyway.

A leader up to 15 feet long would prevent the bright section of line from entering into that circle within which bass are extremely aware of what's going on around them. By using such a rig, you combine the benefit of a high-visibility line where you need it and the concealment of indistinct line close to the lure.

An even better method could be developed by a line manufacturer. It is possible to produce a brightened main line that has as an integral section some 15 feet of low-visibility leader. If you could buy, say, 35-yard coils of such a line-leader combination, you could tie it to dacron or monofilament backing already on your reel. In fishing you could use those small metal clips (no swivel) that many tournament anglers use in order use in order to avoid having to cut the line and tie a knot each time they change lures. In this way you would avoid having to cut back on your low-visibility leader section too quickly. And by the time you had shortened the leader section drastically, it would probably be time to change at least the used 35-yard section. Line becomes burred and knicked after pulling it through enough cover. A 35-yard replacement of line-leader combination would be a lot less expensive than buying an entire reelful of new line.

Innovations like these will help you enjoy the features of both line worlds and avoid situations like one I observed. It happened in 15 feet of sparkling-clear water. I had been on station underwater for some time before my boat-riding angling friend moved in to fish as we had planned. There was a big overhanging lip of bank grass, and several bass were back in where it would be tough to reach them. We were involved in a study of the brightened lines out of their element in the nearly colorless water

My colleague made a cast that hit the grass and bounced the lure into the water tight against the bank. A largemouth swam from beneath the overhang. I could see him stop for a moment. The retrieve started, and the lure swam enticingly out from the bank. The bass started for it right away. Then a funny thing happened. The fish overtook the lure, then moved up on the line, examining it closely. He followed the line maybe 6 or 8 feet before quitting and returning to the bank. There was no doubt that the line had been quite visible to him. It hadn't spooked him, just aroused his curiosity, but he was smart enough to know it wasn't something to eat.

I've seen this sort of thing happen several times. On another occasion a bass charged a monofilament line to which a plastic worm was tied. The worm was lying at rest on the bottom. The fish moved in and stopped a few inches from the line. The worm was twitched, hopped, and crawled. The bass ignored it completely, but he continued to examine the monofilament.

We still have much to discover about how color affects bass angling. One unanswered question that intrigues me has to do with a bass's ability to learn and the inability to unlearn, as reported earlier by Dr. McCoy. Given enough time, you would think that the bad effects of a learned situation must wear off. Maybe not. McCoy has yet to prove that. It makes you wonder if bass caught a number of times on a particular color of lure will learn to avoid that color on all lures. Maybe the fish will avoid the color only on a type of artificial with the specific action that caused the traumatic experience of being hooked.

You've no doubt been aware of the situation in which a new lure succeeds greatly for a season or two and then seems to produce fewer fish. Is it only that the lure's popularity has declined and so fewer anglers are fishing it? Or have the bass been stuck by the lure too many times and thereby learned that it's bad medicine? If so, how do you explain the consistency of purple plastic worms or chartreuse spinnerbaits over the years?

No one is ready to give all those answers yet. But one thing's for sure: To gain a more complete understanding of the behavior of largemouths, we'll have to explore areas besides vision.

4

Sounds That Turn Bass Off and On

When I was a kid, there were still plenty of old-timers around who, if there was too much banging around in a boat on the way to the fishing grounds, would simply turn around and bring the offending big-foot back to the dock. If a novice angler managed to hold still until the fishing spot was reached, then commenced to yap incessantly, the veterans knew how to quiet their guests in short order. If threats of a forced swim failed, the vets would again return to shore.

The old-time fishermen were on the right track, but they tended to overreact in some areas. Though too much talk between anglers tends to break concentration and may lead to other forms of noisemaking, the sound of speech itself is not something to worry about while bass fishing. Such sound frequencies are almost entirely reflected by the water surface. Sound is, however, readily transmitted through solid or semisolid objects. Squeaks, scrapes, bumps, bangs, ticks, and thunks shoot through the water at great speed with an effect similar to having gone through an electric amplifier. Such sounds put every bass within earshot on the alert. Footsteps on a semisolid stream or lake bank also drum into the water and alert rather than attract bass.

To say that bass hear sounds is not enough. Largemouths have the ability to hear fairly distant sounds all right. The bass register closer sounds in two ways: (1) by hearing them, and (2) by feeling them. To get an idea of what that's like, try pinching your nose, opening your mouth slightly so your lips are barely touching, then humming some very low notes. You'll actually feel the vibrations rattling around in your head.

A bass has two sensory organs with which he detects sounds. The first is an inner ear, the second a lateral line. The inner ear is in about the same relative position as our own ear. There is no eardrum as such, and obviously to anyone who has caught a bass, no external ear flaps. Instead, a bass's inner ear consists of a membranous sack within the head. This sack is filled with fluid and contains nerve receptors that transfer sound to the brain.

The inner ear, working in conjunction with the swim bladder, is designed to pick up higher frequencies, but it is doubtful that a bass can detect frequencies as high as can the human ear. Detectable high-frequency sounds seem to alarm bass as well as many other fish. The underwater world is filled mainly with low-frequency vibrations, and it is the lateral line of fish that is designed to register these with extreme sensitivity.

A bass's lateral line can detect frequencies lower than those the human ear is able to register. The lateral line works in conjunction with the inner ear, enabling a bass to locate the precise direction from which a sound is coming. It is also probable that the two organs work together to help bass establish distance to the sound, just as two eyes give better depth perception than one.

The lateral line consists of many tiny openings running horizontally along the bass's body. These openings give access to the lateral-line canals within the fish's body. At intervals within the canals are sensors called neuromasts. The neuromasts connect to nerve fibers, which carry vibrations to the bass's brain. Much more study needs to be done on just how complex and sensitive the combination of lateral line and inner ear is. It would be good, for example, to know which sounds a bass is not able to hear or feel.

We do know that largemouths living in clearer water most of the time depend less on their hearing than do bass in dingy water. Earlier you saw how clear-water bass could not locate minnows in a darkened tank. This is an excellent example of how environment affects a fish's sensory abilities. Most bass fishing, however, is done in dingy water and under such conditions that bass rely quite heavily on their ability to sense vibrations or, if you prefer, hear. So it pays to learn the kinds of sounds that tend to attract or repel the fish, and to consider how accurate their hearing may be.

In the area of accuracy, I don't believe that hearing totally substitutes for the sense of sight. Too often while night fishing I have had bass miss my top-water lures on the first try, as mentioned previously. However, if a bass loses his sight, he may very well be able to hone his sense of hearing to a superfine degree to compensate. Fellow anglers have told me, for example, of catching blind bass that were quite well fed and seemingly quite healthy except for their inability to see. Besides learning to use their hearing to pinpoint prey, such bass learned well which sounds meant danger to them.

Most sudden danger comes to bass from above, and so they are very sensitive to sounds emanating from the area of the water surface. A wading fisherman who moves gently can approach close to bass. So can an angler in a float tube, though the clicking of the plastic foot fins that most fish-tube anglers use to propel themselves can alert bass. Largemouths, in my experience, have not been alarmed by their clicking sound, but they are very definitely aware of it. The use of rubber swim fins is something that more tube fishermen might explore. The one conveyance that permits the quietest approach (yet is the potential sounding board for the greatest noise) is your boat.

Bass and Boat Noise

In a boat you can approach a group of bass with less sound than a ghost settling on a down quilt if you do it right. You can also turn your boat into a kind of aquatic kettledrum and send every largemouth in the area fleeing in terror. The old-time bassing men I mentioned earlier in this section practiced a close-sneak approach in their fishing, and they were in a constant state of anxiety. They always feared that someone would make a noise that would flush all the bass they were sure were just a double pole length away (and often were). Knock a reel against a gunwale and these vets would go off with hair-trigger quickness and let you know of your untraceable ancestry. If aluminum boats had been the only craft

available then, I believe many of them would have given up
fishing. Those veteran anglers, despite their effectiveness, at times
were defeating themselves. But they never knew it.

One of their favorite methods of approach, if the wind wasn't
right to permit a drift into some fishing spot, was with a sculling
oar. "What's wrong with that?" you might ask. It surely doesn't
present the problem of squeaking or rasping oarlocks. From an
above-surface point of view, that's right, which is one reason that
sculling is an extremely effective method of waterfowl hunting.
Underwater, things are different.

A sculling oar, or even a canoe paddle handled in the customary
draw or J-stroke, makes an extreme amount of underwater
turbulence. It's not a sharp sound, like that made by banging solid
objects together, but it's a displacement of water that bass can
sense with their lateral line. When you look up from an underwater
vantage point, you can see the swirls and whirlpools of current
made by each thrust of oar or paddle. A bass doesn't need to see
those whirls. He can hear or feel them some distance away. His
reaction is often to drop into deeper water immediately. Either
that or to work back into the supercover.

Oars or paddles do not provide the quietest way to approach
potential fishing spots. Forceful thrusts of paddles or oars send out
strong stop-and-go vibrations.

Often a far better choice than oar or paddle is the pushpole favored by many anglers who fish the flats off the Florida Keys. Of course if it's your intention to pole up close and fish the heavy cover, then you must plan your approach with great care, moving down from the standpoint position you used while poling, then drifting, then either easing an anchor over the side or tying a line to the pushpole, which you have slowly pushed into the mud. Today we have still another means for a fairly quiet approach to a fishing area. It's the electric motor.

Electric motors have received most of their use by bass anglers. Because these motors are often so successful, many fishermen believe they have no affect on bass. This is not correct. Bass can hear the electrics all right. It's just that in most circumstances the vibrations are not particularly alarming to the fish. It will pay you, however, to keep your electric in slower speeds until you have completely fished an area.

I made quite a few underwater tests by watching the reactions of bass groups while anglers using an electric motor approached and then began to fish in the normal way. I found that when the motors were kept in the lower speeds, the bass would tolerate some stop-and-go sound quite well. But if the fisherman tried to motor quite close and then continued to turn the motor off and on to keep precise position, the fish would usually lose their interest in lures. Sometimes they would sink into deeper water or move back into cover. But first they would all turn and watch in the direction of the motor.

The lesson is clear. If you must constantly use your motor to keep position, stay somewhat out from the area you plan to fish. If you must get close, drift in. If the wind is not right, use a pole for one final thrust, then glide to your spot. All this takes practice. At certain times you can ignore this rule and still catch fish, of course. That's all part of the individuality of bass behavior. Still, the consistency with which this observation has proven true has convinced me to avoid all stop-and-go electric motoring when I must fish almost on top of the bass.

There was another interesting reaction by bass to both a close, quiet drift approach and a more distant approach that incorpo-

rated low-speed stop-and-go use of the electric motor. I still haven't
been able to come up with a satisfactory answer to why the fish
react this way or when they are going to do it. This reaction occurs
when bass of various sizes are in an area. As usual, the larger bass
will have possession of the denser, more favorable (to them) cover;
the smaller bass will be patrolling the perimeter of the cover. At
certain times it seems that the larger bass are just not in the mood
for any foolery or disturbance whatsoever. Even if you use the most
careful of the aforementioned approaches, the big fish slip into
cover or tighter to the cover. If you are underwater watching them,
you can almost hear them snapping a lock closed on their jaw
hinges. There is no doubt about it: those big fish are not going to
eat.

On these occasions, the smaller bass seem particularly fascinated
by the boat. I have seen them move toward the boat and actually
seem to look up at the craft. They are receptive to lures at these
times. Sometimes the smaller bass will not actually move toward
the boat until one of their numbers has hit a lure and been hooked.
Then several bass may follow the fighting fish quite close to the
boat. It is at times like these that another lure tossed near an
already-hooked fish can bring a quick second strike.

Then I experienced days when the younger and smaller bass
would hang back while larger fish (in the 4-to-5-pound class)
seemed more active. The 1½-to-2-pounders would hang back while
the larger fish got first crack at a bait or lure. Yet even though the
larger bass were more aggressive during such periods, they would
not readily swim toward the boat if they were aware of it, as would
the smaller fish.

I was surprised to discover that different types of electric motors
can cause different reactions in largemouths. I worked with a
number of different fishermen with different boats and motors on
countless observation dives. It took quite a while before I finally
began attributing to some motors certain nervous reactions of bass.
It had to do with high frequency again and can partly be
compensated for by using low speeds.

What I learned was that electric motors operating at lower rpm's
with larger propeller blades bother the fish less than those with
small blades (or blades that had been reduced by nicks or wear)

and high rpm's. The noise of your big outboard motor is another matter and must be considered separately.

You can catch bass while trolling with your big motor (or your electric, for that matter). But where you run and how you handle the outboard will determine your success. One of the big determining factors of whether your outboard will spook bass is water depth. If you run your outboard motor over bass that are 20 feet deep, they'll most likely ignore it completely. Even if the bass are only 10 to 12 feet deep, you probably won't spook them (though they may turn toward or away from the commotion of the motor). In shallower water, especially less than 7 feet, bass usually spook or refuse to hit a lure after you run over them with the big motor. If, however, you're not cruising directly over the fish, it is normally safe to ease by in depths of as little as 8 feet, provided you run the motor at a consistent speed.

Consistency seems to be one of the most important factors in determining whether or not bass will spook from a sound.

If you speed the motor up or slow it down, all the bass in the nearby group will be alerted. I've even watched bass in deeper water—as deep as 18 or 20 feet—upset by an inconsistent motor. Normally they couldn't care less at that depth if a motor passes directly overhead. Yet when a boat approached at an even pace to a position fairly close to the fish then had its motor shut off completely, the bass wheeled around suddenly. They all faced in the direction from which the sound had been coming almost as though they were trying to determine where the sound source had gone, and whether it might now be creeping up on them. The reaction is even more marked in shallower water, naturally. Speeding up of the motor produces a similar reaction.

Many bass fishermen have been in the habit of running close to a fishing area at high speed, then shutting down the big outboard before starting up the electric to fish. From what I've seen underwater, this practice is definitely not good. Most bass in the area will be on the alert after a high-speed shutdown.

Inconsistency of sound is probably the reason why bass usually find oars and paddles offensive. Consider the vibrations that a paddle or oar makes. First comes an initial forceful power stroke that gives off strong vibrations. Immediately the vibrations dimin-

Does outboard-motor turbulence disturb bass? Causing this kind of water displacement right up to your intended fishing spot is not smart. It does indeed alert fish, especially when a large motor is shut down. However, low-speed operation (including trolling over bass) does not seem to upset them if the water is at least 10 to 12 feet deep.

ish, then cease, only to be followed by another surge with the initiation of the next power stroke.

Inconsistency, if you think about it, is also the hallmark of a sudden rap or scrape inside a boat. Where all was quiet, suddenly there is a noise followed by silence. Naturally the poor bass are alarmed.

It is fascinating to watch from underwater while a group of bass, seemingly totally at ease, go about their business while an angler's boat floats only a few feet away. When the fisherman in the boat makes a purposeful noise—a scrape, or bang—every fish in the school will spin around and face the direction of the disturbance. On rare occasions, fish will take a bait right after such disturbance or after somebody's run an outboard over them in water of 8 feet or less, but usually they will simply refuse all offerings under those circumstances.

Underwater observation led me to discover one other type of inconsistent vibration that can sometimes put bass off. In clear water so that I could watch the reaction of the fish from as far away as possible, I took up a position on the bottom and waited. Ten minutes later, as planned, my partner eased his boat into position to cast to a group of bass. The fish were holding just out from the edge of a thick snarl of timber. The water was calm, his approach had been as silent as I could have wished, and the fish seemed unaware of him. He had anchored a good long cast away to keep the fish unaware as long as possible.

The first and second casts were with a floating-diving balsa plug. The entry was gentle, the retrieve perfect. I could see no cause for alarm, yet the fish were behaving in an agitated way. They milled about, then began drifting back into the cover. I surfaced and asked for a repeat performance. I bobbed on the surface of the water and watched him cast several times. An idea was beginning to take shape. At first I could not believe that this was the cause for the nervousness of the bass. It took months of seeing the same thing happen before I was convinced.

What had happened was this: Because my partner was anchored some distance from the fish congregation and was using a very light plug, he had to put a lot of energy into the cast. Although there was no scraping or banging of the boat, the angler shifted his weight quickly from one foot to the other as he made a real power cast. His arms whipped the rod hard. The boat rocked with each cast.

The only thing I could think of was a transfer of vibrations from hard casting through the hull into the water. The water was very still, which helped the slightest vibrations to reach the sensitive lateral line of the fish. I'm sure the rocking motion of the boat must have set up small but unnatural wave action in the water.

I later found that if I had the boat move closer and follow all the other steps for a quiet approach, the bass were not nervous at all. Casting was accomplished with ease, so no vibrations from the angler's body movement were being transferred through the boat hull.

I thought back to some of the old fishermen who had criticized my youthful inability to sit still. "It'll ruin the fishin'," they had said. Now I believe they may have been right.

In order to learn which sounds were most offensive to bass, I studied the various noises made 'in boats built of different materials. What seemed to bother the fish most was a tackle box moved over a gritty aluminum hull—a scraping sound. All metallic sounds, whether of oarlock or beverage can on a boat, were bad when close to fish concentrations. You can avoid these noises by learning to move correctly in a boat. It is vitally important to use all your sense of balance and grace and to concentrate on what you're doing. Make your movements conscious until you can move silently without thinking about it. The other important factor, of course, is to sound-deaden your boat and equipment.

Much has been written on this subject, but the easiest and most obvious things are often overlooked by anglers. Boat manufacturers have done a big part of the job for us with the installation of carpeting in most bass boats. Some fishermen have even installed various types of foam padding beneath the carpeting of their boats. Hardly anyone goes afloat any more without soft-sole shoes. But various tackle boxes and trays can still rattle on casting platforms or gunwales, and so can rods and reels. Anglers who use unpadded boats can still benefit from installing on the bottom of their tackle boxes a pad of rubber or foam, or rubber feet. Anchor chains can be covered with plastic, as can anchors. All these things help, but the main thing is to be aware of how you move your boat and how you navigate yourself inside it.

Sounds and Lures

A device called a hydrophone can pick up the faintest under-water sounds. These vibrations can then be amplified, enabling us

Indoor-outdoor carpeting and a boat in which all equipment is stowed will go a long way toward helping you make a silent approach to the fishing grounds. Here, author's son Greg waits for boat to reach edge of clear channel ahead.

to hear them while we're in some comfortable place. The sound waves can also be displayed visually on a chart readout or oscilloscope. Experimenters are beginning to learn that certain sound frequencies are more appealing than others to bass. A few innovative manufacturers are putting this knowledge to use in the design of their artificial lures. An important truth has emerged from this work. In situations where hearing is more important to bass than seeing is, some lures of the same type are more successful than others. Keep that fact in mind when it's time to choose between an original lure that has proven itself and one that is a close copy. Not only may the materials in one be better, one may also have infinitely superior fish-catching ability.

Some confusion can develop when you consider lures of entirely different types. For example, one brand of wobbler may be a consistent producer while another brand of slider is a fish-catcher, too. Obviously they must produce entirely different sounds underwater. And couldn't some lures be entirely silent?

The first answer is that bass, on different occasions, seem to prefer different *types* of sound. Second, you should know that all objects moving through the water make sound—maybe not sound as you and I understand it, but sound-making vibrations nonetheless. A hair or feather-tail jig swimming slowly, occasionally touching bottom, tree, or rock or coming through weeds, will produce sound that the hydrophone can pick up. Even a plastic worm crawling over the bottom makes sound. If you were underwater with me listening, you couldn't hear it either. But those lures make vibrations that can be amplified enough for us to hear them.

The obvious question is: can bass sense those vibrations without having them amplified?

Scientists are now trying to find out. Chances are good that a bass's lateral line is capable of picking up the vibrations made by even the quietest of lures. How else do you explain a largemouth's ability to crush a deeply sunken plastic worm that's easing along a weedline at night? He may get some slight shadowy visual indication of the lure, but not in the way he would if you were working the artificial on the surface.

What is emerging from the scientific work is that bass have

several areas of sound-frequency preference. You might classify some of these as low-slow frequencies: sounds such as those made by worms, lizards, jigs, some spoons, and grubs. In the higher, faster frequencies of preference are those made by spinners and various plugs.

Most good spinners throb out their messages with force that's easy for bass to sense. Plugs are another matter. Some plugs have wide, lazy-swimming movements; some have extremely tight wiggles; some fall between the two extremes. All plugs give off slightly different vibrations (sound frequencies). In my experience, plugs with the faster, more-potent vibrations do the best job when bass want a lure that sounds off. Otherwise, the low-key jigs and worms are more successful. In other words, *no middle-of-the-road lures.*

Another approach that seems to interest bass to the point of attack is to alternate casts: cast first the more violently vibrating lure, then the quiet lure.

Why should a bass even attack an artificial lure in the first place? Sure, today's lures are quite realistic. But to me, they still don't quite look like a real fish or other form of prey underwater. You might think a bass would be a little more discriminating than he is (or maybe you think he's far too discriminating already).

I have watched with fascination while countless numbers of various lure types were working underwater. From these observations I have come to believe that consistency is the factor, again, that is largely responsible for triggering a bass to strike artificials. Lures are inconsistent, and in this case, that's good. Let me explain.

Earlier you saw how a consistently running motor (as long as the water was not too shallow) didn't bother bass. It was the inconsistently run motor that alerted him. The same principle holds true for feeding behavior. When bass are not actively feeding, forage fish can safely move close to them. The little fish swim easily without frightened movements near the largemouths. The forage species, however, seem to sense when a bass is about to start feeding again, even if they don't see the jaw-popping routine that largemouths often go through prior to feeding. When they get the danger signal, little fish that have been virtually tickling a bass's belly quickly leave.

Now if you were to present an unnaturally moving or ailing forage fish to a group of bass that were not actively feeding, you would most probably start something else going.

An injured minnow or shad does not swim evenly—consistently. Its movements cause erratic vibrations, which attract bass and other predators. The strong vibrations of lures do much the same thing. It takes the erratic vibrations of a spinner or plug to trigger bass that are not actively feeding. But then how do you explain the effectiveness of jigs and plastic worms in nonvisual situations? Most jigs and worms, although they do not produce vibrations from some built-in action, are generally effective in dingy water when they're worked with a jump-type retrieve. Those jumping movements certainly produce underwater sound.

The reason that inconsistent lure action attracts bass is very simple. To a largemouth, the action means a frightened and easy meal. Bass become excited and attracted. You hope they'll strike. Sometimes it's only the last erratic twitch or sudden jerking motion you give a lure that pushes a semiactive or nonfeeding bass into actually striking. Never fear that you can jerk a lure too fast for a bass to catch. If he really wants it, he'll get it.

During the many hours I spent watching lures retrieved underwater, I tried to psych myself into the fins of a bass—to really imagine myself being able to react only like a largemouth. A psychiatrist would certainly have a field day with my mental processes, but then he'd probably have something to say about fishermen in general anyway.

Regardless of my abilities to imagine that I was a bass, I can tell you that I became fascinated, totally entranced with the little dancing lures that happened by. The ones that really intrigued me were those that came merrily along and then either: (1) took a great hop near me, or (2) paused for just a second before suddenly picking up speed. I found myself wanting to reach out and grab them.

In your own experience, the same sort of big hop or pause followed by a speeding up of the lure has probably accounted for some good fish. Of course my experiment was based on visual reaction; I couldn't hear the lures. But I believe a bass responding primarily to sound reacts about the same as he does when he visually follows lures. In other words, if he hears something coming closer and it suddenly tries a panic escape when it's nearly in front of his nose, why he'll naturally want to grab it.And it's the erratic sound of an injured minnow that does the trick.

You can perform your own experiments abovewater to test the effectiveness of an inconsistent retrieve. You need a rod, a reel, a practice plug with no hooks, and a cat. Different cats will respond in various ways, but cats are good volunteers because they are like bass in many ways. A kitten is more active. An old cat is a lot harder to interest. Cats seek cover like bass and also seek out comfort. Both creatures respond with extremely fast reflexes and spook easily, and neither one will point a bird or fetch a duck. You can learn a lot about bass by watching cats.

Practice outdoors, making casts with the rubber practice plug near your cat, which will no doubt be basking in the sun. Try different kinds of retrieves. Usually you will find that it is the teasing, more erratic retrieve that gets Tabby out of that sunny spot and chasing your moving plug. Again, that's a visual response, but the reaction of the bass to sound vibrations is very similar.

Erratic movements by injured baitfish (or lures) give off what are known as distress vibrations. Injured forage minnows also produce an alarm scent, just as it is believed bass do. Distress vibrations affect bass just as they do sharks in salt water. The reaction is widely known. Live-bait anglers cause bait minnows to produce such inconsistent movements by clipping various fins. Based on experience, the season, and the local weather trend, experts can predict with great accuracy whether a situation calls for a single pelvic fin clip, a pectoral and pelvic clip, or a dorsal clip. Each causes the minnow to produce a different action and degree of mobility. Bass may want a fairly helpless bait one day and one that can move with moderate speed another.

Many anglers are sold on spinnerbaits whose blades are adjusted on a wire arm to occasionally hit the lure's own lead head. It is said that this arrangement gives the lure even more erratic action than a normal spinner. Up close underwater, I believe I was able to catch a scant moment when a blade might have touched a head, but maybe it was wishful thinking. I do know, however, that such lures at times have caught fish while others similar in every other way did not. The lures are definitely noisier.

Built-in rattles have made a lot of anglers and tackle makers happy. I do not know how near the lure must be before bass hear a rattler. I cannot hear a rattle plug further than about 18 feet. If the rattles do add to a lure's fish-catching ability, then I think it will be under very poor light conditions—at night, or in very dingy water. So far I haven't personally discovered any advantage of rattle lures over nonrattle lures—in fact in ultra-clear water, bass actually spook from rattle lures—but then I don't have the lateral line or ears of a bass.

The sound of a surface disturbance is a very obvious attractor for bass, as it is for all predator and scavenger fish from sharks to catfish. I'll never forget the first time I tried to wash my hands in the Gulf of Mexico off the Coast of Mississippi after an evening of fishing for spotted seatrout. I splashed my hands, and suddenly the water erupted as a huge school of sea catfish (hardheads) churned the surface white in an attempt to nibble my fingertips. I might add that my fingers were hastily withdrawn.

Bass are not quite that aggressive, however, and it is possible to overdo your surface noisemaking with lures. Underwater, I've seen largemouths turn completely from lures that were worked too energetically. Sure, a popping plug chugging like an in-tune percolator will catch bass sometimes. But you'll have more consistent success with such surface lures if you concentrate on swimming, vibrating, and only occasionally popping them. This is especially true by day. At night you can be a little noisier.

While on the subject of surface sound, it's worth mentioning that the old myth of knock 'em on the head with your lures has about outlived its usefulness. If you've fished a lot for bass, you know that such tactics can spook largemouths. It's practically always better to cast just beyond where you believe the fish are holding, then bring your lure back past the probable holding spot. You can also cast to the side and then bring your lure back so that it will run in the proper place—in front of the fish. Though from time to time you'll catch a fish by casting right at them, bombing bass is not a best bet.

The visual stimulation of actively feeding bass causes most bass in a group to begin feeding, as we saw back toward the start of this chapter. I now believe that the sound of a school of bass tearing into baitfish on or near the surface can also stimulate other bass to feed. The competition factor is operating.

The first inkling I had that this theory could be true occurred on big Toledo Bend reservoir. Bob Stearns, one of the nation's top all-around anglers, and I were in separate boats. I was casting and catching fish from a small group of young schooling bass that were tearing up the surface. I turned around to needle Bob, whose boat was maybe 50 yards away, and I saw that he was also fast to a fish. The strange thing was that I could see no sign of schooling activity.

The same sort of thing happened again and again at closer and greater distances and in widely removed spots. Sometimes both of us would be into schooling fish; other times only one of us. At first I thought that the bass school was just huge and spread out or broken up on two groups of shad. But as the distances grew greater and Bob and I still hooked up at close to the same time, I began to suspect that the explanation was something else.

On different lakes and at different times, I found the same sort of thing happening. I finally began to study the speed with which vibrations travel in water. I learned that the sound of one group of schooling bass can travel through the water at the rate of something like one mile in one second. How far such a sound travels is still questionable. I'm convinced, however, that the sound of largemouths schooling in one area is enough to stimulate into feeding another bass group that can hear but not see the first.

How can you put that information to use? Very simply. Let's say you're working over one schooling bass population and catch enough for the fish to break off feeding. If you know of another good holding area fairly close by, head directly for it. There's a good chance that the bass will have become active in the second spot simply because of the feeding frequencies broadcast by the first group. This parlay won't always work, but it works often enough to be worth investigating.

We have seen how largemouth bass translate sound frequencies into defense reactions or into feeding behavior. Fish of all kinds are involved in other kinds of sound that they create themselves.

Biologists classify these sounds as mechanical or biological.

A tropical or semitropical ocean is the noisiest of underwater worlds, but even a fresh-water lake is not silent. Fishermen can hear only a small portion of the sounds that occur in our fresh-water rivers and lakes. Perhaps the most startling of those noises is the drumming sound made by the fresh-water drum during its mating season. This sound plus tooth grinding, bone rubbing, grunting, and groaning are the sounds biologists call biological noises. It is believed they are all an attempt at communication between fish.

By contrast, the sounds that fish make when eating, sucking air from the surface, chasing bait, or spawning are dubbed mechanical noises. Thus far it has been determined that largemouth bass and various panfish make several groups of noises while spawning. Though it has yet to be determined in which category these sounds belong, scientists have found that if spawning sounds made by the panfish are recorded and reproduced at a time other than the spawn, they tend to attract these little gamesters. The same should hold true for bass. I wonder if it would be possible to produce a lure that would vibrate with the frequency of those sounds?

There is a man-made kind of sound that, depending on its intensity, seems to intrigue or frighten largemouth bass. For lack of a better label, I've named it the rumble phenomenon. I had really been aware of it all along, but I'd just forgotten some lessons I'd learned as a kid. Friend and fellow diver Jim Gregg brought it all back.

On a warm late-spring day, I was back in the boat after a session underwater. While I was warming up in the sun and tending to the fishing, Jim and another fellow were seeing to the diving chores. The sun felt wonderful on my back. A hedge of dense brush and trees ran along the lake shore beside the raised bed of railroad track. By and by I became aware of the distant rumble of an approaching train. The sound grew louder, and soon the engine flickered into view behind the foliage. A string of freight cars followed. Suddenly Jim's head popped into view.

"Cast over there," he said, pointing excitedly. "There's a small pod of fish that just woke up. They're milling around like crazy."

He then spun around in the water. "You can really hear that train," he said.

With that he ducked under again. I wasted no time throwing my lure where he had indicated. I took several fish in short order. Then I started remembering.

I recalled a long-ago time at a northern New Jersey reservoir where the kids used to crawl under a fence to fish. One of our favorite places was a willow-shaded point where we'd pull in fat bluegills. Just to the left of the point was a concrete railroad bridge. For some reason that day I had worked around the point and was casting a little silver spinner along the bridge abutment when a train came rumbling from the north. It had not quite reached the bridge when a strike stopped my lure short. The fish bore down, then came up in a splendid leap that made me start shaking. I guess I had a right to be excited. It was my first bass. A smallmouth, and not a very huge one, but a bass nevertheless. I remember much later that day thinking that maybe the train had something to do with it, though I couldn't imagine what.

Some years later I read a story about a kid who confounded his elders by catching largemouths with unbelievable regularity from a bridge. A train bridge. His action seemed to coincide with the passage of trains. Then I started thinking about all the other fish I'd caught around bridges—trout, crappie, pike, and probably others I'd forgotten.

It wasn't only trains that seemed to have an effect. I began finding some correlation with the passing of big trucks—the semis were best—on automotive bridges. There seems to be something in the vibrations of such machinery that excites most fish, including bass. It will pay you if you're fishing near a bridge, or a place where train tracks or highway pass close to the water, to put forth a special effort when locomotives or trucks begin an approach.

As my underwater work on bass continued, I discovered that not all loud abovewater vibrations produce favorable reactions. I have fished in a lake where major road work was in progress nearby. There was blasting with dynamite not too far away. The sudden explosions, though not close enough to bother our ears underwater, seemed to frighten the largemouths. They would make sudden darting movements, and they were quite unwilling to be caught at such times. Another phenomenon that seemed to put them off was the sound of a jet plane breaking the sound barrier nearby. Again, here was a sudden noise rather than a gradual increase of vibrations.

All together, sound plays an important role in the lives of largemouths. Anglers who fail to consider it in their fishing will obviously still catch fish, but perhaps not so successfully as someone who is careful to avoid those vibrations that offend bass and take advantage of those that please them. Fishermen who insist that the bigmouths are still there even after they scrape a tackle box or knock an oar are probably right. The fish may be present, but chances are that they won't bite.

5

How Bass
Strike Lures

The strike of a largemouth bass is one of the most accurate in the
fish world. Muskies, walleyes, pickerel—none of these predators can
match a largemouth once he has homed in on a target. The strike
of a bass, besides being accurate, is fast and violent.

If you have fished long for largemouth bass, you can undoubtedly recount instances when the fish displayed no such positive
behavior. Probably you have had days when the bass picked at
your lures like an anemic canary. You have probably also had
times when they charged up full of sound and fury, only to go past
your carefully worked artificial with never a touch. If you should
ever observe bass underwater and see just how many fish actually
follow retrieved lures without striking them, you might be even
further convinced that the bass is not nearly as aggressive as he is
usually described. Your impression would be inaccurate.

If a bass really wants a lure or bait, you'll have a difficult time
keeping it from him. The problem is that we are frequently not
presenting these fish what they want, when they want it, and how
they want it.

In order to gather information that will turn more follows into
hits, I've spent many hours observing largemouths as they strike
lures underwater. I've come to the following conclusions:

· Largemouth bass strike various lure types in different ways.

· Environmental conditions determine how a bass will strike one
given lure type.

· A bass's physical condition affects how he will strike a lure.

· Bass size and season of the year influence strike response.

· As in other areas, individualism plays an important role in just how a bass will strike a lure.

Before we get into these points one by one, let's borrow a trick from the trout angler. Fly fishermen have learned well the importance of matching their imitations to the type of insect the trout are feeding on at the moment. The same principle applies to fishing for bass.

One of the first things to do when you're about to fish a new lake or river for largemouths is to learn the various forage species in that water body. Though largemouths will sometimes take a strangely colored or shaped lure, the most consistent success will be had by anglers who use lures that closely imitate (in size, color, and action) the natural forage in the lake.

If bass have lately been feeding heavily on free-swimming prey, they may be slow to respond to bottom-crawling lures or bait. The reverse can also be true.

Each time you go onto the water, it's vital that you determine the right retrieve. Bass, because of prey movements and weather conditions, can quickly change the way they want their food. When great amounts of forage become available, for instance, it is more difficult to tempt largemouths with artificials unless the fish are tearing into a school of baitfish.

Now let's look at the variables that determine how and why bass strike, and how those factors affect your fishing techniques.

I watched bass strike many of the more popular lure types before I came to a few conclusions that will probably punch holes in some cherished myths about bass fishing. I'll begin with how bass strike soft-plastic lures, for they are probably the most popular lures used in today's fishing for largemouth bass.

Soft-plastic Lures

The main categories of plastic lures include worms, lizards, and grubs. Most plastic worms traditionally have been designed to resemble earthworms, even though to the best of my knowledge you never see nightcrawlers swimming around in the water. The newer plastic crawlers have departed from tradition, incorporating various tail styles and unique body structures, and that is good. If you think about it from the viewpoint of a bass, the long cylindrical shape of worms probably represents eels or various salamanders. Such creatures are predators upon bass eggs as well as natural forage for largemouths, giving wormlike lures a double-barrel impact as bait. The plastics may also resemble snakes.

The plastic worm has been around for quite some time now. But it has only been the innovation of the so-called curly tail (which undulates through the water) that has been responsible for a change in the way we've begun fishing all types of plastic crawlers. The change has been for the better.

The old raise-and-settle method of fishing a plastic worm will take bass, but it is far from being the most effective. In most cases,

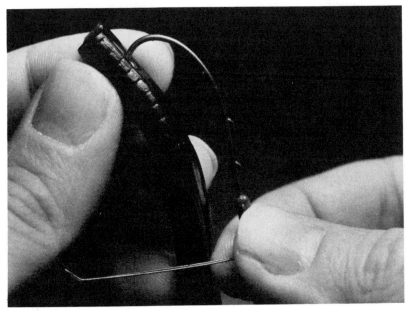

Here, in this and three following photos, is one good way to rig a plastic worm with a wire-weedguard hook. It's a little-known trick that puts the hook eye *inside* the worm head rather than outside in front—a chief complaint about wire-weedguard hooks. First, insert point as shown here in *side* of worm head.

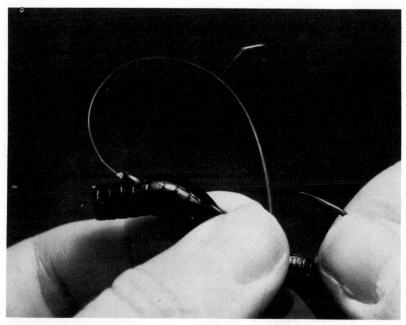

Work the hook shank down, and push the point and barb free. Your line must already be tied onto hook. Finally, bury the eye in plastic and push it forward slightly inside worm.

especially in normal (dingy) bass water, it is the faster-swimming retrieve that takes more bass. Average bass.

For the very biggest fish, the best retrieve seems to be a fairly swift hop-swim action. Big bass are also likely to hit a plastic worm as it is dropping—frequently just after it has entered the water on your first cast to a holding spot. Many anglers miss these takes because they are not prepared to strike the instant the worm enters the water. In this situation, a bass will not hold the worm in his mouth for longer than ½ second. You can prepare yourself to turn these strikes into hooked fish by employing the following technique:

First, you should close your spinning-reel bail or engage your levelwind reel the moment the worm you've cast touches the water. At this point you must keep all slack from your line by raising your rod tip slowly. This technique is often referred to as backpressure (or tightlining your lure as it sinks). It is the only way to see your line twitch (frequently the only signal that a bass has grabbed your

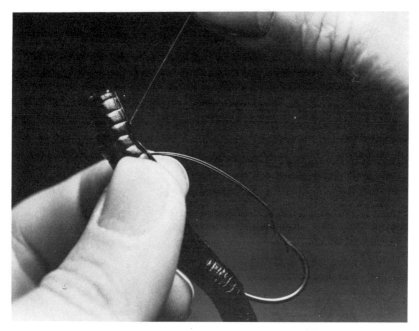

Now rip the line through the soft plastic so that the line comes out at center of head.

crawler), or to feel the slight tightening of line or sharp tug that indicates a bass is there.

You should be aware of the water depth in the various good holes you'll regularly fish. In this way, should your line stop settling at 3 feet, for example, when you know the water depth is 7, you'll be alerted to set the hook immediately. If you do not receive a hit on the initial drop, then commence the hop-swim or swimming retrieve.

Usually you have no doubt when a bass hits your swimming worm. You feel a sudden thunk. Your reaction should be to strike quickly. More often, though, you'll experience the familiar subtle tap-tap sensation or (if you've been concentrating on the line where it enters the water) you'll see your line kick. This action will occur when the worm is dropping after a hop. Here's what's happening underwater at these times:

By the time you receive the tapping message, a bass will more than likely have your entire worm in his mouth. In the old style of worm fishing, we believed it was best to give the largemouth slack

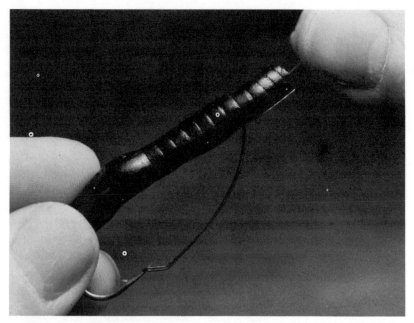

Here is the rigged and finished result. The hook eye is inside the worm head.

and let him run for a few moments before we struck. We caught bass this way to be sure, but only because the largemouth was among his fellows and made a run in order to prevent other bass from stealing his worm.

If a bass is not being pressured by his fellows, he'll usually do one of two things:

• When he has the worm in his mouth, he'll maul it. If you let him hold that artificial for too long, he'll detect something wrong and expel it. Therefore you should strike immediately upon feeling that tapping sensation.

• Or a bass will grab a plastic crawler, blow it out, inhale it, blow it out several times. What he is doing is trying to kill the worm. Your signal that this is happening will more than likely be line twitch. Too often fishermen wait until they see several twitches before attempting to set their hook. This is a good way to miss a bass. Often the fish is really not interested in eating the worm, but only in destroying the eel-shaped predator to their eggs. After a couple of quick in-and-out gobbles, the bass has had enough.

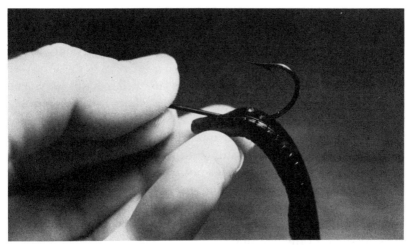

Another trick with worms involves using a straight (not offset) hook. This and the following photo show how. A lot of anglers like the straight-shank hook because it is available in small thin-wire sizes. To rig it in the weedless manner and still have the worm straight, insert hook point as shown here, into the side of the head rather than the front. Point comes out ½-inch down body.

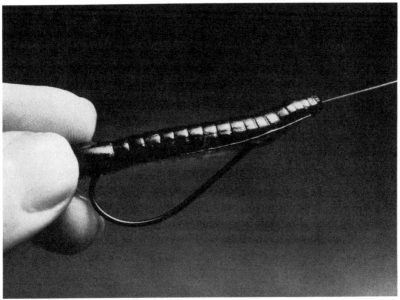

Hook point is then inserted into body of worm in the normal way. Here's how the properly rigged worm looks.

Satisfied that the threatening creature is dead, the bass cuts off the attack.

For you to be successful when bass are striking this way, you should train yourself to strike with a short, sharp stabbing movement (as opposed to a long sweep), the instant the line twitches the first time. If you miss when using this short setting movement, your worm may still be in the action zone and the bass may hit again. If your worm has not become wadded on the hook from the setting action, you may get a second chance. If you do connect by using the short stab, hit the bass again to make sure the hook is in. If you've been a trifle slow and have waited past the ideal moment of the first line twitch, be prepared to hit at the very next movement of the line—if it comes.

Contrary to popular belief, bass do not take a worm only from the head end or (as other stories have it) only from the tail end. My underwater observations of bass striking plastic worms showed that largemouths will attack from any angle. They'll be more likely to take in and expel the larger worms as just discussed; the smaller worms will most often be mouthed entirely. The most difficult strike to turn into a hookup occurs when you are using a slip sinker of ⅜ ounce or heavier.

What happens is that the bass grabs your worm and then darts off at close to a right angle. The cone slip sinker stays put. When you try to set the hook, you must first overcome the inertia of the sinker. The result is likely a missed fish. Because of this problem, many fishermen are now sticking a small section of wooden or plastic toothpick into the hole of the slip sinker. Such pegging keeps the sinker up snug against the worm. A jig head or one of the worm weights with metal eyes at both ends will give you the same advantage. There's no need to worry about whether a bass will take a worm well because he feels the weight of the sinker. As long as the sinker is not too heavy, a bass will take it up along with the artificial. With an integral hook weight, you'll stand a far greater chance of hooking up.

Sometimes bass do nip at the tail of a plastic worm. Frequently these are small bass. Such a strike will be felt as a rapid *rat-a-tat-tat*.

Panfish, too, nip at a worm like this, causing the same sensation. To determine which species is after your worm, switch to a small (3½- or 4-inch) worm. If it's little bass, you should soon catch them.

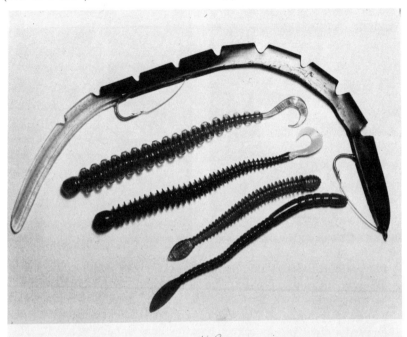

Worms for bass are available in a great variety of sizes. Top to bottom: the giant Hawg Hunter used by Florida trophy fishermen, next the Action Breathing Worm, then two Rebel Ringworms, and finally a Sweet Willie worm. The Breathing and Ringworms capture air bubbles, which are expelled during retrieve. Small worms are becoming more popular because they catch both little and big bass.

On some days, bass are so skittish that they'll spook the moment a lure hits the water near them. Sometimes they'll even move out while the lure is still in the air. Plastic worms or lizards are the best choice to use on those days when you observe the wakes of bass fleeing from cast plugs or spinners. A small jig presented by flipping it with an underhand movement is also good in such situations. The key is a quiet, gentle presentation with a lure that

Bobby Martin (left) and Johnny Morris (right) demonstrate two different methods of setting the hook when using plastic worm. Martin prefers spinning tackle. He sets the hook by yanking on handle of spinning reel as well as rod. He is right-handed. (When he used a revolving-spool reel, he sometimes ripped the handle off after striking many fish.) When he uses spinning gear, his rod is always in his stronger, faster hand. If he used a conventional casting rig, he would be holding the rod in his left hand during the retrieve. Johnny Morris, by contrast, prefers conventional casting rig, has never experienced handle trouble, and prefers to come back over his shoulder a little more (as shown in photo) than Martin does while setting hook. Martin gives a little whiplike snap of rod tip while setting hook using plastic worm. Morris drops down for a fraction of a second, then sets. Two different styles for setting the hook using the plastic worm. Both work. The main trick is that you must be fast, responding immediately to the strike.

offers only a slim profile. Your retrieve should also be a slow swim with gentle (not sharp) hops. This quiet approach is also one to use in clear water.

There is no doubt in my mind that largemouths in clear water respond to plastic worms differently from the way bass respond in dingy water. In my experiments, I watched while worms of various colors descended near good bass-holding places. Those bass that were interested would rush over, assume a head-down attitude hovering over the worm, and watch it carefully. If the worm were hopped in clear water—which normally produces good strikes in dingy water—the largemouths would turn away. If the worm were raised slowly, then made to swim, sometimes the bass would strike.

But the retrieve that best induced strikes in the clear-water situations was performed like this: Let the worm remain motionless on the bottom for a few moments after it settles. Next, crawl it forward no more than ½ inch. Pause, then bring it slowly forward again that short distance. Keep this slow retrieve going, and very likely one of the big fish that has been hovering over the plastic crawler will crash down, nail the worm, and veer away.

In the early spring, from the time bass start to engage in their spawning activities, until early May in the South, and as late as June in the North, a different plastic lure will take more fish than will the worm. The lure to try is any plastic lure that resembles a lizard in shape. When using a lizard, you must be even faster in reacting to a strike. A largemouth doesn't hold a lizard in his mouth for even the short time that he holds a worm. The sole intent of the bass is to kill this egg predator.

When a lure resembling a lizard approaches, all bass become extremely alert. In striking a plastic lizard, a largemouth shoots forward and drives the lure into the bottom. He'll go down into the timber or weeds and crush the lure so hard that the corners of his mouth will flare out white. As soon as he senses that he's mangled the lizard, he'll expel it and back off. The action happens like lightning. The only way to hook fish consistently when they are attacking lizards like this is to keep slack from your line studiously and set the hook the instant you suspect you feel the slightest difference in the way the lure is reacting underwater.

Plastic-tail grubs and feather or hair jigs are also excellent early-season lures. You can use jigs as small as those normally used by crappie fishermen. During the pre-spawn period, which is marked with erratic warm-cold weather, I've had excellent success using jigs as light as ¼ to ⅛ ounce. As the season grows old, however, you should fish the larger grubs.

The difficulty with using jigs and grubs is that bass can take them so gently that you may never become aware of the strike. Largemouths don't really strike a jig. A bass positions itself close to the jig and flares its gills to pump the lure into its open mouth. When the bass do this, a bit of line moves in, too. That movement is often telegraphed as line kick. As an alternative, you may also receive a slight sensation of slack. When you're using a light line, either of these two reactions may be your only indication that a bass is taking. It helps if you keep reminding yourself that a bass will be taking the jig or grub as it drops rather than as it's moving up. With all this, you've got to accept the fact that you still will not hook fish on every strike.

Not only does experimental psychologist Don McCoy study the ways of bass, but he is also an excellent bass angler. Once I watched underwater while he threaded a tiny crappie-size jig down through a tangle of timber to where a group of huge largemouths were holding. It was a bright sunny day and these fish, so deep beneath the supercover, would have been impossible to reach through normal casting. Using a modified "flippin' " technique such as that made popular by Dee Thomas, Dr. McCoy jigged and gently vibrated his little lure as near as possible to the big fish. Soon a Goliath of a fish shot toward the lure. He paused inches away and in a single movement opened his mouth and flared his gills. The jig disappeared in the fish's mouth. I wanted to yell to Don. Then the big bass pumped his gills once more and the yellow jig flew out.

I asked McCoy if he had felt anything.

"Not a thing," replied the good doctor.

No matter how fine your concentration and reflexes, bass have a habit of doing such things to you with disgusting regularity. It helps greatly if you're using a jig heavy enough to hold your line straight. A jig that's too light will let the line hang in kinks or coils. While it's possible that the straightening of a line coil could indicate a taking fish, I believe you have more control over your line and lure the tauter your connection between the two.

Plugs

A bass will hit a plug from nearly any angle. If he strikes it at the head end or side, you'll generally have no problem feeling him. If you've cast so that a bass must come out to catch your plug from behind, your only strike sensation may be a quick feeling of weightlessness or a sudden pause in the vibrations from the swimming plug. When a largemouth attacks from behind, he can (even if he is only of moderate size) move up on the lure, take it into his mouth, continue swimming in the same direction, and finally expel the lure without your having the slightest idea what was going on. If you're tuned to that momentary weightless feeling and strike right away when you detect it, you will probably surprise yourself by catching fish.

A largemouth bass can perform this engulfing maneuver on a plug that has two—even three—sets of treble hooks, and he doesn't need a great deal of swimming room to do it. He can engulf your underwater lure as it moves past a stump or weedbed, and in all probability you will think that your lure has picked up a piece of debris when you feel the vibrations check for a moment

Bass also seem particularly excited by plugs that bounce off rocks, timber, or pilings during the retrieve. Some lipped or billed plugs, because of a particular quirk in their design, seem able to bounce off objects—without becoming fouled—more easily than others. The sudden change in direction caused by a caroming plug evidently triggers a reflexive strike reaction in bass that are not really inclined to hit otherwise. The rebounding lure may resemble a fleeing forage fish.

A plug that has fouled its hooks together can also produce sudden strikes. The plug is usually twitched on the surface until the hooks are free. On the next twitch the lure dives with its normal action and also frequently elicits a strike. Similarly, I've seen large bass that were holding beneath mazes of downed timber respond once a plug caught its hooks on the springy branches. As a fisherman snapped his rod tip trying to free the plug, the erstwhile uninterested bass would grow extremely excited. Their dorsal fins would become erect, and one or two fish would shoot toward the branch-snagged lure. But the moment the plug snapped free and wiggled off normally, the fish became uninterested once more. The erratic action of the fouled plug probably resembled a helpless forage fish, or just possibly a shad that was spawning.

Bass seem to become familiar with plugs that are used regularly in an area. When the bass are feeding vigorously, this limitation doesn't seem to matter. But when you must muster all your skill in coaxing a fish to strike, it's better to experiment with a type of lure or plug that hasn't been heavily used in that area.

As we've already seen, bass from a clear-water environment rely primarily on their vision to home in on lures during the daylight hours. During one underwater experiment when the fish seemed intent on devouring every lure we presented to them, the bass refused to pursue a particular fat type of plug that was a very popular seller. It was difficult to understand what could be wrong. During subsequent experiments, we finally discovered the problem. The plug was equipped with a rattle, as are many popular lures. When a plug identical in every way except for the noisemaker was tried, the bass began to attack it.

What has come from these experiments is the conviction that bass lures that send out extremely potent sound frequencies are not right for bass in clear water. In dingy water, such lures are often excellent, giving the fish a target to home in on before he can see it.

Spinnerbaits

The popularity of the safety-pin style of lure is deserved. These baits enable a fisherman to work a thick maze of timber, a stump field, or fairly thick vegetation without having to free his lure every 6 feet during the retrieve. Yet when visibility is good, largemouths will not follow spinnerbaits as far as they'll follow plugs, worms, or jigs. Spinnerbaits are most effective in muddy water on individual bass rather than groups of bass. Spinnerbaits are excellent when loner largemouths are holding far back in a hole or within a thick network of stickups. These bass make their living by responding quickly to prey that enter their holding territory. They respond much like trout in fast water that must decide quickly whether to strike before a morsel is swept away.

Bass that respond to spinnerbaits are normally reacting to the sudden appearance of the flashing object, the clanking and then vibrating of the large blade, and finally the enticing wiggle of the skirt when they have nearly reached the lure. These fish do not

The spinnerbait is not the all-around lure that many bass fishermen have cracked it up to be. It is excellent around heavy timber and some vegetation. Bass hit it from ambush in a reflexive attack. But where a bass has plenty of time to follow it, the lure is not so effective. When the spinnerbait is used properly, it brings tail-walking results such as shown here.

have the opportunity to line up the lure before striking. They strike from any position, so they may be coming at the lure from an awkward angle. The result: sometimes they don't become securely hooked.

Anglers often sense that the bass are striking short when this happens. Their solution is to add a so-called trailer or stinger hook to the main hook of the spinnerbait. The large eye of this second hook slips over the barb of the main hook, and the trailer is held on by one or two small rubber or plastic washers. The system works but it is primarily because a bass attacking suddenly from an awkward angle has less chance of missing two hooks. It's best to let spinnerbaits drop into holes in cover, then bring them steadily out. With this type of lure, a jerking, erratic retrieve is not as successful.

Shiner Minnows

Bass are likely to hold on to natural bait like minnows longer than they would most lures. Still you mustn't think that shiner fishing is a snap. This is a demanding type of fishing, yet one that once mastered will result in catches of more larger bass. Largemouths can strike a shiner any of five different ways. If you use a bobber, you'll be able to determine most of what's going on. Here's the way it looks underwater.

• A bass can move in, grab a shiner, and swallow it. That's the simplest form of strike upon natural bait. It occurs mainly on the smaller minnows or medium-size shiners that, luckily, are taken the right way, head first. The strike is usually signaled in this way: The bobber suddenly goes down. It may start moving off, but not always. If you set the hook immediately, you'll usually connect.

• In the second strike form, the bass intends to kill the shiner quickly and be done with it. In this type of strike, the largemouth will take a shiner any way he can, crush it, then blow it out. Your bobber will signal such a strike by diving suddenly, usually moving a couple of feet, then popping up just about the time you're setting the hook. It's maddening. The best thing to do is let your shiner remain where it is. Possibly the bass will take again. If he does, set the hook immediately.

• The third type of strike is similar to one way a bass takes a plastic worm. The largemouth grabs the shiner from any angle, mauls it a moment, expels it, then takes it in again several times. The fish is doing two things: (1) he is killing the bait, and (2) he is positioning the bait for the final swallow, which will be in a head-first direction in order that the fins and spines of the forage fish will not choke him.

During these maneuvers your bobber will be dancing, kicking, going under briefly, then popping up. Though it can be difficult for you, the only way to hook up now is to wait until the bobber finally goes under and stays down. It's possible that this will not happen, that the bass will finally just reject the shiner completely. Still you have your best chance if you wait until the bobber submerges before you drop your rod tip a moment and then set the hook.

Bass will handle hardshell prey like crayfish, crushing it and expelling it several times before actually taking it down.

• In the fourth type of strike, largemouths sometimes take a shiner quickly and then run with it. They're doing so to avoid other bass that attempt to take the bait away. You can gamble that the bass has taken the shiner well and strike in the early part of the run. Or you can open your bail or put your levelwind reel into free spool and let the bass go. If everything works out well, the bobber will come up again and commence those dancing movements that signal that the bass is mauling the bait. Wait until the bobber goes down once more before striking.

• The fifth type of strike happens if a shiner or Caledonian minnow moves into a bass bed. A guardian largemouth will grab the intruder and immediately move the bait out of the nest area. Do not wait to strike in such cases. When the bobber goes down, you should drop your rod tip and then set the hook right away in a powerful upsweeping motion.

Environmental Conditions

We have already seen how bass are often spooked or at least refuse to take rattle-type plugs in extremely clear water, and how it is best to move a plastic worm only a fraction of an inch at a time where visibility is great. There are several theories about such situations. I believe that when bass hover over a plastic worm in clear water, they can be spooked by a sharp hop if the worm is attached to a very bright monofilament line. As far as the rattle plugs are concerned, bass in clear water probably mistake plugs for forage minnows from some distance. It is completely unnatural for a minnow to make such a rattling noise, so the fish shy from such a lure when they can see it first.

I've also noticed in my underwater observations that it is the first presentation of a lure—especially in clear water—that stimulates the greatest curiosity among bass. Subsequent presentations result in progressively more negative response. More on that later.

In water with poor visibility, largemouths home in on sound first. When they finally see the lure, it's in a flash. Usually they're committed by then and do not discriminate about size, shape, or color, knowing only that here is some vibrating creature that must be easy prey. Bass are conditioned to respond this way in all their natural feeding.

When you begin to get into deeper areas (15 feet or more), water clarity ceases to be such a critical factor. Here the color of line, line size, and lure finish are not as important as they are in shallower water. Bass in deep water will strike things they would not normally take in the clear-water shallows.

In all environments, however, it is important for you to keep your presence unknown to the fish for as long as possible.

Physical Condition

Most bass fishermen are aware of how the changing seasons affect largemouths: faster metabolism in warm weather, slower metabolism in winter. It's only recently that I've become aware of condition cycles within a season. Glen Lau brought my attention to one of the early-season peculiarities that follow spawning. After the spawn, bass enter a recovery period, during which it is impossible for them to strike a lure. We'll discuss this phenomenon in greater detail under life cycles, but for now it is important for another reason. During the months that follow the spawn, mature largemouths go through what might be described as up and down periods. When they're in a period of high or prime condition, they're physically able to run down just about anything they want to catch, even bluegills. Normally a bass has difficulty capturing bluegills in a free-swimming situation.

During a low period, the bass are relatively dormant. They either suspend themselves in the water or lie near the bottom. The baitfish seem to know they're not threatened. They approach bass with no concern. At times, the turned-off largemouths might make a token effort—especially after spawning—and move toward a shiner, but the forage fish can easily outdistance the bass.

During the high cycle, bass will feed heavily for four to five hours. Sometimes groups of fifty fish will feed en masse. These high-low cycles occur on an average of about every fifteen days throughout the year. During the warmer weather, a high occurs more often; during the early spring and winter, less frequently. These cycles are affected by local weather extremes.

Lau described an experiment he performed on some bass that were being held in captivity for observation. These fish were accustomed to being fed at a certain time. During a period of warm, stable weather in what was a low cycle for the fish, he threw in some shiners and watched those bass that responded at all. They came slowly up and struck where the bait had been. The bass could be caught with bare hands.

Even during high cycles when bass are feeding well on readily available prey, excessive fishing pressure can cause the fish to move their home areas, unless there is a good deal of supercover nearby.

Southern California biologist Michael Lembeck, who has done much work on the San Diego lakes, is another scientist who has experimented with telemetry—in which tiny transmitters are imbedded into the bodies of bass. His studies showed that bass in deeper water or very heavy cover would stand greater fishing pressure. Eventually, though, the deep-water bass would move if too many lures were worked past them.

Bass Size and Seasons

Why is it that on some days you seem able to catch nothing but smaller bass? Part of the answer no doubt lies in the tendency of larger fish to hold in the hardest-to-reach places, as we've seen in earlier chapters. This pattern leaves the smaller fish roaming the edges of the best cover, where they're more susceptible to a lure.

Another reason is the cycles that we've been discussing. Remember, it is mainly the mature fish that are affected by these condition cycles. Don McCoy, whose experimental work on bass has already been described, has another interesting concept.

"Though it is yet to be proven," says McCoy, "it may very well be that learning to inhibit a strike response is something that develops slowly in bass." We give old lunker-size largemouths credit for being plain smart. Maybe that's so, but it also may be that these fish just happened to survive to the stage when they are able to withhold strike response, an ability that the younger bass possibly have not yet developed.

Another thing for consideration is the size and availability of forage. During later summer, when baitfish are plentiful and of larger size, bass do not need to eat as frequently. A short period of gorging will sometimes suffice for as long as a couple of days, even in warmer weather.

As mentioned earlier, it pays to match your artificials in size and finish to the available forage. As the season progresses, you may consider using larger lures. In heavily fished areas, however, there comes a point where smaller artificials can often produce more fish.

The smaller spoons and jigs are excellent to use for vertical jigging through branches of downed trees and other cover. They are good in both cold and warm weather. Top tournament angler Bo Dowden specializes in using 2½-inch-long spoons that weigh only ⅛ ounce. He prefers the lures for use on bass that are suspended. The little spoons tend to flutter down and stay in front of the fish longer than would heavier, more streamlined lures.

Dowden tends to use the light spoons in clear water. In dingy water he'll normally choose a tailspin type of lure and tightline it down (as previously described on page 64); making a good deal more vibrations than a spoon.

Though repetitive presentations are not usually the key to success in most seasons, during cold weather it takes largemouths that are holding in deeper water longer to react. So it pays to keep a lure or bait working in their vicinity.

After one tournament victory, California angler Dave Gliebe told how he was forced to work a jig-'n-worm combination up and down, over and over to elicit strikes in the cold water of early spring. The bass had moved up under a mat of vegetation that had a slight depression beneath it. Once one bass struck, the action seemed to excite the other fish. Often several would strike right afterward, close to the boat.

For this cold-weather deep-water fishing, sinking crank-type lures (the divers) reeled slowly, dropping tailspin-type lures, and jigs and eels are right.

B.A.S.S. Masters Classic winner Rick Clunn demonstrated another twist to cold-weather fishing. At his first top-honors win of the Grand Prix of bass-fishing tournaments, Clunn proved that though slow is often right in cold water, there are times when a fast retrieve can do the job also. To glean a bunch of his fish, Clunn worked a diver-type plug down into a hole, then stopped cranking. Just as soon as the lure halted, the bass hit it.

Rick's other fish were taken on a spinnerbait. The lure was not worked as a slow-dropping or "fall" bait, as many anglers fish spinnerbaits in cold water. Instead, Clunn buzzed the lure just beneath the surface, the blades bulging the water that barely covered them. He used big blades—one of them with a copper finish, the other brass. The key was that the fish were in fairly shallow water in milfoil. One reason Rick was able to elicit strikes despite the cool weather is that shallower-holding fish are more aggressive than deep-water fish.

Seemingly minor elements can make the difference between moderate success and a grand slam during the various seasons of the year. Minor variations in lures are another example. I've already mentioned the success of plastic salamander imitations over plastic worms in the early spring. Another fascinating example was revealed to me by Glen Lau, who had observed how spawning bass respond to harassment from bluegills. The bluegill is by far the worst enemy of bass beds. Schools of them surround a bass on the nest, awaiting the opportunity to dart in and begin devouring the eggs. What triggers the guardian bass is usually a single bluegill. The first panfish to take a head-down attitude triggers the largemouth's instinct to protect or kill. The bass will charge the bluegill, though he seldom catches it. In the meanwhile, of course, other bluegills move in and start decimating the nest.

Lau designed a lure that duplicated the head-down bluegill movement and found that it was very successful from early to late spring. The plug behaves like this: It comes wiggling through the water until you stop it; then it ever so slowly tilts its nose down and begins to descend. It drove the bass wild. Most lures come wiggling through the water in a similar way, but once you stop them they either float, remain suspended, or sink with a slightly tail-down attitude.

At first, Lau tried merely clipping on a little weight ahead of the nose of a standard floating-diving plug. The head tipped down too quickly. Finally the film maker tried flat lead strips, the type often used by fly fishermen. He hammered the strips into cuts in the lure to get the proper effect.

"One day while I observed underwater," reports Lau, "we caught every bass we cast to using this lure."

The artificial sank at a rate of about one foot every 15 seconds. It was a slow-wiggling lure that was best worked on light monofilament. Its success is just one more proof of how important it is for you to seasonally select your lures. In other words, it's important to imitate the forage that's currently available.

Here's another example. After spawning time in Florida, big salamanders (known locally as sirens) ply the weedbeds close to shore. These 11-to-13-inch beauties are pounced upon by big bass and some smaller bass that ought not to be so greedy. It is during this period that the huge 13-inch plastic eels start to become so effective in this part of the country. Whether you like to fish a surface lure or soak a minnow, if you think about it I'm sure that you'll be able to find some situation in nature that you are in harmony with when your favorite method is most successful.

Individualism

At the very beginning I mentioned that bass, like other animals, are individualistic. No matter what behavior you learn as being typical for the species, more than one individual fish will break the rules. Individuality also shows itself in the way bass strike.

Most bass will regularly attack lures any way they can. But some individuals will constantly trail a lure or bait, striking or nipping only from behind. Cautious, I guess. Some bass are extremely aggressive. They never seem to learn restraint. They'll strike a lure just about anytime it's presented to them. In waters that are hard-fished by anglers who keep the bass they catch, these exciting, aggressive individuals are sadly few in number. Naturally: they're the easiest to catch.

The less aggressive or maybe smarter or just more cautious bass are caught, too. These fish often seem to learn—if we can use that word—from the experience. After they are released, they're hesitant about taking an artificial for some time. The question is, can they influence other bass?

There's no scientific answer to that question yet. However, tackle manufacturer and tournament angler Tom Mann insists that at least one bass he knows of can keep its fellows away from artificial baits. Mann keeps a huge (18,000-gallon) aquarium stocked with largemouth bass, crappies, white bass, and channel catfish. One bass in the tank goes by the name Leroy Brown. Mann calls Leroy the smartest bass he's ever seen and insists the largemouth will nudge out of the way any other bass in the tank if the newcomers seem likely to take a lure that Tom is working in the aquarium water. Leroy may really be protecting his fellow bass. He could also just be going through token competitive behavioral responses that in a natural environment would end in his swiping some of the feed, too. Yet Tom Mann tells how Leroy went to a dying bass in the tank, a fish called Big Bertha, and tried to nudge her upright when she fell over onto one side. Leroy stayed with the dying female all day, and when it was finally over he swam back to his corner of the aquarium.

I've seen times when the only thing that started a group of bass feeding was competitiveness. That competition was triggered by the aggressiveness of one fish. The others in the school would be hanging quietly. Then one would dart out and nab a shad or other baitfish. It was all that was needed to start the others gorging.

Some bass, when they grow to over 7 pounds, become loners, taking up station in some hole or other. Yet I've seen many of these larger bass in groups. These fish were together in holding areas, not just schooled for feeding. Small bass are supposed to be the "schoolies" and often are. Yet as often as I've seen schools of yearlings, I have also observed singles and pairs of fish that size swimming unhurriedly along a dropoff.

There are territorial bass—the homebodies—and there are the roamers. Within both those categories are individuals that help make bass fishing the fascinating and confounding sport that it is.

Positive and Negative Responses

When you cast a lure to a bass lair, a fish that is lurking there is going to respond in one of several ways.

His negative reactions can include any of the following:
· No movement whatsoever.
· Turning away from the lure.
· Actually moving away or fleeing from the lure.

His positive reactions can include any of the following:

· He can turn and watch a lure passing through.
· He can move slightly toward the lure, then stop or follow it at a leisurely pace for quite some distance before turning away.
· He can swim deliberately, quickly after an artificial before breaking away.
· He can strike.

Many factors stimulate a positive response. Most or all of them must be working together to result in a strike.

A bass must be presented with something that will give the impression of either the natural forage he is accustomed to eating or the natural enemies of his spawn.

In this rarely photographed strike, a largemouth shoots from his weed cover and devours a plastic worm that was being worked along the bottom.

This imitation or natural bait must be presented in a way that duplicates the normal manner in which his food or enemies arrive.

The lure or bait must not be encumbered with detractive features. It should have the right finish and be on a line of the right weight and color for the water conditions.

The lure or bait must be presented at a time or in a way that elicits a strike. The most obvious time is when the fish is hungry. Or the lure or bait must be presented to trigger the competitive instinct: close to another hooked fish, for example. If you're fishing heavy cover, then you're appealing to a bass's reflex reactions and your presentation must be right on target, giving the fish no time to follow but only to react.

Avoiding negative responses can be an even more complex subject, but there are a few main points that will help you overcome the things that seem to turn bass off. Even among the anglers who have studied largemouths for years, there is some disagreement on this subject. Most fishermen agree, however, that repetitive casting with the same lure (a technique that eventually triggers an Atlantic salmon) is not the way to go with bass. Because

This largemouth flared up from its holding position beneath a log after a bright fat-type plug and is about to be boated. Anyone who doubts that a boat or its occupants are visible to a bass in clear water need only to examine this photo, which was taken from underwater.

of my underwater observations of many bass and their various responses to lures, I agree fully. Hammering the largemouth over and over again with one kind of lure will normally either put the fish off or ultimately send him from the area.

Some anglers are so cautious of instilling a negative attitude in the fish that they will cast only one lure one time into a good holding area. Others, once they take a fish from a spot, will not cast to the area the rest of the day. These practices may be fine if you have unlimited cover and fish to work during a given day. But few fishermen can afford to operate that way. What makes more sense is alternating the types of lures or bait that you present to fish in one area.

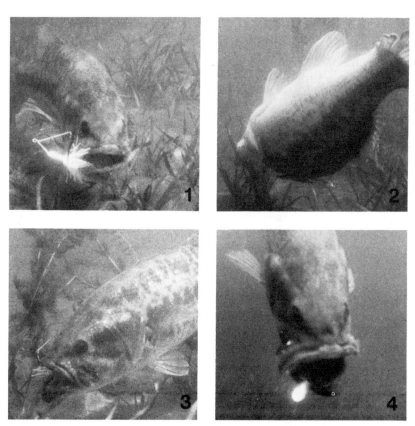

Spinnerbaits trigger reflexive strikes and subsequent fights such as the one shown in this sequence. This bass had little time to follow and examine the lure.

Top bass fishermen like Rayo Breckenridge of Paragould, Arkansas, and Tom Mann of Eufaula, Alabama, are both advocates of the alternating-lure theory. Rayo once won a B.A.S.S.

Masters Classic by using crankbaits followed by worms. Tom, unlike some fishermen, will fish a hole for quite a while if he's sure the fish are there. He may work an hour in one spot that he believes the fish must be using because of environmental conditions right then. If he takes a fish on, say, a plastic worm, he won't necessarily continue hammering away with that lure. He may switch to a tailspin type of lure. When he takes a fish on that, he may very well switch back to a worm, but this time in a color different from the one he was using earlier. Then he could change back to the spinning lure but work it differently, maybe tearing it quickly through the water.

Film maker Glen Lau believes very strongly in *not* showing bass the same lure over and over again. Yet his approach is somewhat different from Mann's.

Glen selects five or so lures that have been consistently good in the area he'll fish. They may include a fat-type wobble plug, a floater-diver plug, a plastic worm, a spinnerbait, a surface lure, and maybe even a flyrod bug. The lure with which he starts depends on the precise cover he is fishing, the season of the year, the weather, and how the fish have been feeding in the past several days.

One thing is certain: Lau will not cast more than once with one lure if he is sure some fish are holding in a particular spot. If you cast one type of lure in, a bass may turn and watch or follow that imitation without striking. Not enough of the positive response factors just discussed were present. Now if you cast that same lure back again two or three times, the fish may examine it. But usually that's as far as they'll go. If you then were to toss in even the lure that incorporates all the right factors for the particular situation, the bass would not hit it. As Lau describes the situation: "Their sharp responsive edge will have been worn down. They're far less likely to be triggered into striking."

But if you had changed lures after that first cast, trying others of those carefully selected for the situation, your chances for a strike would have been excellent. If several bass are in the holding area and one does strike, it is very likely—because of the competitive factor—that others will then be stimulated to strike. If another angler is with you, he can take advantage of this behavior and cast near your hooked bass as the hooked largemouth is brought in. True, this technique can lead to fouled lines, but it can also result in a fast hookup with another fish.

Lau maintains that to pound an area with the same or very similar lures over a period of days will ultimately teach the bass rejection. They should not be taught rejection or they will become extremely difficult to catch.

On the other hand, as we've seen, cold-weather anglers have learned that continually working an appropriate lure in front of a bass concentration will very probably produce strikes. In these circumstances, the largemouth's metabolism is at such a low point that it takes a good deal of time for the fish to be able to respond.

When conditions are very difficult, the multiple-lure concept can be expanded to incorporate natural bait. Here you are actually simulating a natural feeding situation and appealing to the instincts that cause bass to tear into schools of forage fish, which occur in summer and often in fall. Make sure, however, that this use of bait is legal in your state.

What you do is toss a few unhooked crippled bait minnows into the hole you plan to fish. You might follow this with a flyrod popper or light balsa minnow plug, which are twitched like the naturals. After you take a bass or two, try a plastic worm. This sudden change in feed is usually enough to hold the interest of the largemouths. Also the plastic worm is an excellent lure. Next switch to a natural minnow as bait. Make it a fin-clipped minnow that cannot move too far from the area. If you take another bass, try a minnow that is in excellent shape, one that is quite lively.

While you're fishing the different lures and baits, toss a minnow or two into the hole from time to time to help keep the bass alert. By the time you have caught and released several bass and have reached the frisky-minnow stage, it's likely that any other largemouths will have become pretty wary. This method can at times produce truly wild action.

I've seen bass kept in an excited striking state for some time through this alternate use of natural bait and artificial lures. When the bass are in a positive mood to begin with, you need not start with a live minnow. Use your artificials until things get slow. I know from my underwater observations that the fish will be sinking down to the bottom or moving back into heavy cover if you hook and keep a few of their fellows. All it takes is a few shiners or other small fish thrown in to perk up their interest again. Once they see a couple of their buddies chomping down on real live minnows the others will be ready to strike once more. Finally they will reach the cutoff stage. Then nothing you can offer, including natural bait, will make them strike again. As earlier mentioned, if you continue to pressure them they are very likely to leave the area. If you are releasing bass and one of those you put back is injured, it will often spook the others. All of which brings us to the consideration of another point:

Can bass relate the unpleasant experience of being hooked to something you do as a fisherman? If so, can they later refuse to strike because of this "knowledge"? We looked at some of these things earlier in this and other chapters, and it is obvious that new lures or a time lapse between sessions of fishing a particular group of bass is conducive to better angling results. Some anglers believe that bass have a strange telepathic ability to communicate their unpleasant experiences to others in a school. There have been, to the best of my knowledge, no scientific studies to try proving or disproving such a concept. I do know, however, that a bass can relate an *unpleasant* experience to various elements in its environment. These fish can also relate various stimuli to *pleasant* experiences. Don McCoy's color experiments with a food reward are an excellent example. Bass can also be trained to respond to underwater sounds that are a prelude to feeding. On the negative side, bass learn that various man-made sounds or sights indicate danger—or the unpleasantness of being hooked.

I know of one obvious instance involving a group of largemouths in a small lake. They had received virtually no fishing pressure as we know it today. The first bass boat equipped with a high-whining electric motor fished the area with excellent results. Seen from underwater, the bass didn't show evidence of alarm at the sound of this fishing motor. All bass caught were released. After a couple of days, whenever the fish heard the electric motor approaching, they would sink to the bottom or ease back beneath logs and other thick cover. They had obviously made the connection between the sound and being taken from the water.

Tackle

The technique of casting different lure types on successive casts (or presenting a particular lure in precisely the right place and proper manner to produce the kind of positive response we're looking for) must be made simple. Otherwise, fishermen will not try it. Fishing practice will, of course, improve your presentations. But don't overlook a streamlined way to make the alternate-lure concept work. Your tackle is the key.

First of all, you can be sure that no one is going to cast a lure once, cut it off, tie on another for a single cast, and so on until the five or six artificials chosen for a particular spot have each had their inning. One option is to use one of those little no-swivel clips at the end of your line, but not everyone is happy with them for use on all lures. Also if you use this arrangement, you are still not doing everything possible to achieve the best presentation.

Ideally you should have three—possibly four—rods and reels with which to work various types of lures. For example, the rod you need for fishing a plastic worm is exactly opposite from the rod needed for ultra-light balsa plugs. And the rod that nicely pitches those light plugs would not be right for most spinnerbaits.

It is not only for *presentation* that you need a rod matched to the type and size of lure you're pitching. A properly balanced tackle outfit also permits you to *retrieve* your lures with ultimate sensitivity. You must know whether your lure is vibrating correctly, or if you have a slip of weed impaled on your hook point. A rod that's too stiff or too heavy will also deaden your sensitivity to what the lure is up to. A line that's too heavy will keep a light lure from descending properly. Line that's too light will hold a medium to fairly heavy lure through part of a cast, then snap in two and let the artificial sail high out over the water and be lost. And that might have been the lure that would have brought old bucket-jaw from beneath a log in an explosive elastic-mouth strike.

The appropriateness of spinning, fly-casting, and bait-casting (levelwind) tackle for bass is a subject for endless discussion. Each has a definite place. You are limiting your success if you insist on using only one type of equipment.

Take the flyrod, for example. In many parts of the country, fly casting for bass is synonymous with springtime and popping bugs. Yet fly casting is right for bass at certain times in every season except winter. I have learned that in the mornings and evenings of midsummer, a little deer-hair or elk-hair mouse or moth of the same material dropped gently into pockets is frequently the only lure that will trigger a strike. A long flyrod is perfect for flipping plastic or natural worms back into small holes in supercover. The same rod can be used to cast or flip small natural minnows into areas that are impossible to reach with anything but a canepole. Streamers are very effective bass lures, but they should be tied on weedless or semiweedless hooks. And the streamers must be as large as the forage minnows in the area, a detail that many fly casters seem to forget.

I use both bait-casting tackle and spinning tackle for bass fishing, assigning them to different tasks.

I normally cast all my light balsa plugs and small jigs and mini-plastic worms with spinning gear. The spinning rods I use are short—5 feet or under—but they have a great deal of back-bone.

My favorite casting rods for use with bait-casting (levelwind) reels, are from 5 to 5½ feet. I use this tackle for all standard plugs and most plastic worms.

For casting and fishing large shiners, I use both spinning and bait-casting tackle, but the rods are at least 6 feet long.

I use no ultra-flexible rods for bass fishing.

Depending on the environment, I'll go down to line that tests 6 or 8 pounds. The heaviest line I use for normal fishing is either 10- or 12-pound test. For some of the shiner fishing with heavy-butt, 6-foot-long rods, I'll go as high as 30-pound test, though I prefer 20. This is my personal choice. I know some very successful bass fishermen who use as much as 40-pound test in some cases and never go lower than 17. You'll have to make your own decisions based on the water you normally fish.

The main point with tackle is to become proficient in all the methods and learn when and why particular equipment is best for the various situations you will face.

6

New Lines on the Natural History of Largemouth Bass

Bass have been called the most successful all-around predators that swim. If we include the oceans, I'm not sure I agree. Unlike other highly successful fresh-water predators, such as the northern pike or muskellunge, which are built for long-range speed, a bass is built for extremely fast, short bursts of motion.

Take a look at the next largemouth you catch. Notice that the fins run along most of its body. For their size, largemouth bass have a high ratio of fin surface to forward body section. This design makes them extremely maneuverable at high speeds. They can move in any direction—even backwards for a foot or two. Compare this fin arrangement with that of the pikes.

The great size of his mouth enables the largemouth bass to engulf a variety of prey. With age, that mouth and the skull in which it is set become even more pronounced. The head takes on a high hump or peak shape; the lower jaw juts fiercely. If an old-time bass reached human size, meeting up with one underwater would be an unnerving experience. Besides being a nearly perfect predator, the bass has one other attribute that makes him an extremely successful biological creature: the ability to adapt to varied environmental conditions.

This adaptability enables bass—like man—to spawn, feed, and

grow in a wide variety of situations that stray quite widely from theoretically ideal conditions. Bass survive the winters of Quebec in the northeast extreme of their range and the broiling sun of Central America in the southwest extreme. Contrary to popular belief, bass have a broad spawn tolerance range.

Spawn Factors

Largemouths can spawn in a variety of depths and temperatures. In one study at Bull Shoals Reservoir, bass spawned between 55 and 78°F. at depths that ranged from 2 to 17 feet. Largemouths seem able to spawn successfully over a wider variety of bottom types than other bass species. They can bed on loose sand after they sweep it clean down to harder bottom. They use gravel, tree roots, stumps, some types of vegetation, mats of algae, and compacted soil. The thing that seems more important than the bottom type or consistency is the existence of some kind of cover nearby. The main reason for this need of cover is to enable guardian bass to protect their offspring from the ravages of predators—the bluegill being by far the worst.

An overpopulation of bluegills in a water body can virtually eliminate natural largemouth reproduction. Hordes of stunted bluegills will eventually eat most of the bass eggs, and there seems to be another factor:

Recent studies of human populations have shown a seeming drop in fertility among city dwellers. Theorists believe that stress from crowded living conditions stimulates hormonal activity that effectively cuts down the number of children conceived in many urban areas. Fish biologists believe that when largemouth bass are stressed by bluegills, either a chemical or mechanical stimulus takes place that inhibits or at least partially suppresses bass spawning. Some studies show that in such crowded situations the spawning is suppressed by the male bass, even before nest building. The crowding doesn't seem to affect the bluegills at all, except to keep their size down.

Much of what has been written about bass spawning and even

pre-spawning is less than accurate. And yet some of the new facts about the species that have been gained through actual underwater observation should not be considered the final word on the life cycle of largemouths, either. Though largemouth bass have been observed by me and others in widely varying geographic areas, doubtlessly there are other bass that will do things differently. Once again, the individual fish and different populations must be taken into account.

It is important, though, that we consider some of the things that can and often do happen that, according to a few of the old bass myths, supposedly never did happen.

For instance, the moon and sun and their various interactions were once thought to be the sole predictors of bass actions. This notion was not long ago disclaimed by many fresh-water fishermen, but now new interest in the various theories has sprung up. I still maintain that nothing beats becoming extremely familiar with all the whims and intricacies of the water you regularly fish. I have found, however, that the moon, as it relates to the natural function of spawning, plays an important role. Most bass spawning behavior begins to occur when the water reaches the high 50's F. and is rising. Bass have spawned in much colder water. All the preparatory activities prior to the actual spawn usually occur during the days and nights building up to the night of the full moon. If an extreme cold front should suddenly move in—a distinct possibility in the early part of season—the bass very probably will curtail their pre-spawn activities until the next full moon.

When conditions are finally right, bass that have held off spawning for one or possibly two months (if weather has been bad) become extremely active when they're finally able to consummate the reproductive act. The biggest problem with bass that have been forced to endure a long cold spring in which they've cut short their spawning several times is this. When the fish are finally able to complete the spawn, the date is late. This situation usually results in the female's depositing all or most of her eggs in a very short time, possibly in just one or two nests. When the temperature of the water is in the 70's, a female largemouth may deposit all her eggs in something like half an hour or fifteen minutes.

Some bass anglers specialize in sight fishing during spawning season. Here Dennis Rahn scouts for nests. He will try to catch male bass (which he releases), then female if she is still near the nest. He does not bother with bass under ten pounds.

Also of great importance is that the late-spawning bass in warmer waters seem far less concerned with their nests than are early-spawning bass. Guarding is minimal, and therefore a less successful spawn is to be expected. The best conditions for spawning, therefore, consist of cool to mid-range temperatures (high 50's into the 60's) on the rise during the week building to the night of the full moon.

Courting Behavior

Several fascinating kinds of bass behavior occur prior to spawning. Though I have observed some of them, film producer Glen Lau has credit for observing more types of behavior during this period than anyone else I know. Lau has categorized five separate courting procedures of largemouths, which follow on the heels of the now well-known stage (usually six days before the full moon) when the female bass congregate at concentrations of underwater timber, where they rub and bump themselves. Though no one knows for sure, it is believed that they do this to loosen the eggs within their body cavities.

During the actual courting procedure, individuality takes over again.

· In one type of courtship activity, a male bass will choose a female and stay with her for as long as nine hours. During this time he will bump her, nudging her toward the nest he has already prepared. Other males bite the females hard, actually putting marks on their nose in a ferocious display of lovemaking that takes place prior to the spawning act. If the spawn time is late and the water warm, this courting period may occur for only a brief period, perhaps a quarter of an hour.

A second type of courtship takes place two or three days before spawning. The male goes to the area where the females are gathered at the rubbing timber, chooses a female, and then moves away with her. The two swim the shoreline. They'll cover half an acre easily before choosing a site. I have seen pairs of bass circling probable sites for some time before deciding against them and moving elsewhere. The spawn site may be by itself or part of a communal spawning area comprising many nests. The male builds the nest and then entices the female over it.

· Multiple spawning occurs when two or three males and females all spawn in one nest. However, one dominant male and female will remain to guard the hatching fry.

· There is a fast courtship that occurs when an aggressive male first fans out the bed, then swims out to collect a female. He may travel up to 200 yards to find a mate. Once he does, the two swim right back to the nest, where spawning takes place. There is no period of swimming the shoreline together.

· A rare type of courtship might be called role reversal. In this situation, the female picks the spawning area she desires and then waits for the male to happen by. When he does, she darts out, bites him, nuzzles him, and finally corrals him. She may move him 20 or 30 feet to the area where the nest will be constructed. The male, during all this attention, is quite docile. Then a change takes place. Maybe it is because of a temperature change, the warmer shallow water raising the male's metabolic rate. Or maybe he just becomes tired of the female's bullying. In any event, now he becomes the aggressor, rushing at the female, who coyly darts away. The male will then build a nest and eventually get his female back for spawning.

Spawning and Guarding Bass

In some water bodies, bass use the same area for spawning year after year. In other lakes, different places are chosen each year. It depends on how the environment changes and also upon the population of largemouths present—whether they are great roamers or resident types that like to take up housekeeping in a small area.

Another myth-breaker relates directly to the spawning act. It has been assumed for some time that the male bass fertilizes the eggs as the female expels them. Not true. The male largemouth is alongside the female while she deposits her eggs, but he is just guiding and supporting her over the nest. The female tilts to one side to expel the eggs. (A healthy young female may produce 4,000 to over 30,000 eggs during one season.)

Soon after the female is finished, the male bass moves over the eggs. He lowers his tail, sweeps with his tail, and exudes the milt to fertilize the eggs. The tail-sweeping movement helps deposit the milt more evenly and spreads and juggles the eggs to receive the milt.

Another fondly held belief was that the male bass drove the female from the nest immediately after the spawning act. This is not so with largemouth bass unless multiple spawning (just described) is taking place on one nest. The female largemouth remains near the nest at least twenty-four hours—at least with Florida bass. She takes up an outer perimeter guard post while the male bass remains over the nest, fanning it with his tail. Almost all the successful nests are guarded by both the male and female bass; the most successful nests are those near which the females have remained the longest.

By and by the female will lose interest and drift away into deeper water to recuperate. The male stays on guard at least two weeks, sometimes longer. One strongly held belief is that the male

This bass has a nest just below the visible rock and is not at all afraid—only annoyed at diver and his camera.

bass'immediately begins devouring his young as soon as they hatch because he is so hungry from fasting while on guard. Not true.

Aggressive male bass has nest far back in hole to rear. The curving weeds above and at two sides give nest good protection. Bass here rushes out at Gibbs in anger, turning away from the diver-photographer only at the last moment.

The male bass remains with his young as they hatch, through the period when the yolk sac is still attached, through the fry stage until they are approximately ¾ to 1¼ inches long. One of the more difficult things for the male parent is to stay with the cloud of tiny fry as they begin to dart about. It is difficult enough to keep predators from the eggs, but if a school of fry splits or spreads out too much, the male bass cannot protect them all.

When the little bass reach the fingerling stage, they're about three to four weeks old. They have fully formed scales with mucous protection. At this stage, they begin darting into thick vegetation for cover. It is well they seek cover. At this stage, everything— including the male parent—wants to eat them.

The young bass grow through the warm weather until their expanding appetites force them from the nursery within the shelter of vegetation. When they emerge, they're prime targets for all predators, including larger bass. The youngsters are usually no more than 6 inches long when they leave the protection of the heavy vegetation. Those that survive are constantly alert—and lucky. A survival rate of one out of a thousand young to reach maturity is good.

Post Spawn

What happens to the adult bass just after spawning?

A lot of fishermen have by now realized that the period immediately after the bass leave their beds can be extremely unproductive for fishing. Such poor results seem to go against logic. Shouldn't the bass be very hungry after spawning? Well, they probably are. But also they're so fatigued that it's impossible for many of them to capture forage. The larger females are the bass that most fishermen would prefer catching, but just take a look at what happens to these fish after they spawn.

The female largemouths, after their time of guarding the nest, drift into deeper water or open pockets in vegetation. Or they may be suspended between the surface and bottom. They hardly move. Some are tilted to one side. They seem nearly dead. Only one gill, usually the one on top, moves. There is very little fin movement.

These fish cannot pursue any forage. Some of the bass in this condition ultimately die. Fortunately for bass fishermen, most of these fish recover. After recovery comes a period of moving into late-spring and early-summer holding areas and patterns, and the fish once again begin to feed.

Of course not all bass are in this recuperating stage at once, so you'll be able to catch at least some fish when you believe most spawning has just ended. In fact, most places have several spawns a season, involving different bass groups. But post-spawn bass fishing is generally tough.

Growth

Young largemouth bass grow at extremely varied rates. Much depends on the available forage, which depends on the growing season, which in turn depends on the local weather and man's manipulations. Bass spawned later in the season may never reach the size of those spawned early in the year. By the end of its first year a young bass can be 3 inches to nearly a foot long. The Florida subspecies of largemouth bass, which ultimately can grow much bigger than the Northern largemouth, shows obvious growth differential from the Northern variety at least by the time they have lived a year and nine months.

The weight difference between the two bass tends to be accentuated with age—especially over the prime growing period of the bass. Not all Florida subspecies of largemouths, however, grow to great trophy size. There is a wide range of size, even among the Florida subspecies as well as other hybrid bass strains. Overall, there seems to be far less growth variation among individuals of the Northern strain of largemouths.

Another fascinating fact is that young largemouths, in their early stages, may school with the species that later is to become its archenemy—the bluegill. On numerous dives, I have watched bass of 5 to possibly 6½ inches acting as though they belonged with the bluegills—or sometimes red-ear sunfish. Not only do the bass swim along with the bluegills; they also readily feed near these sunfish. I have never seen more than a few young bass at a time with the bluegills. It may be that the remainder of the schoolmates of these young largemouths were devoured earlier in the game, and that the survivors wisely sought the protection of another school—even of a different species. This is only a hypothesis, but I have no other explanation for such behavior.

During the cold weather of winter, bass grow little or not at all. We have seen how largemouths will take a lure—especially one jigged vertically near timber around which a largemouth school is holding. Largemouths do feed during the winter. But it has become obvious through stomach analysis that a small winter meal lasts a long time. In fact, the metabolism of bass is so low during winter that an individual fish may consume a minnow no more often than once every two weeks.

That sounds like depressingly low odds for winter anglers. But the good news is that the slowly jigged lure often elicits a reflexive strike, even though the bass really doesn't need to eat. So your chances for a winter bass are really much better than they might seem at first.

An interesting, recently discovered fact about the Florida strain of bass is worthwhile mentioning at this point. In recent years there has been much interest in introducing the Florida subspecies into waters outside its natural range. The bass's inclination to grow so large makes it extremely desirable as a sport fish. With a history of bumbling experiments involving the introduction of species that should never have been, today's aware biologists are going slow with the Florida subspecies. One of the chief fears concerns this bass's supposed inability to survive harsher winters than those that normally occur in Florida. If the Florida bass were to crossbreed with native Northern bass and this feared genetic sensitivity to cold water were passed to offspring, then many bass in a given water body would die.

The winter of 1976–77 provided some insights into just how much cold these Florida-strain largemouths could survive. In captivity, healthy individuals of the Florida subspecies have endured 39°F. water temperature in fine shape. But the fish must be healthy to begin with. If not, if they're fatigued from one cause or another, they will not survive such cold water. Normally it takes over thirty days of severe cold water to begin affecting healthy

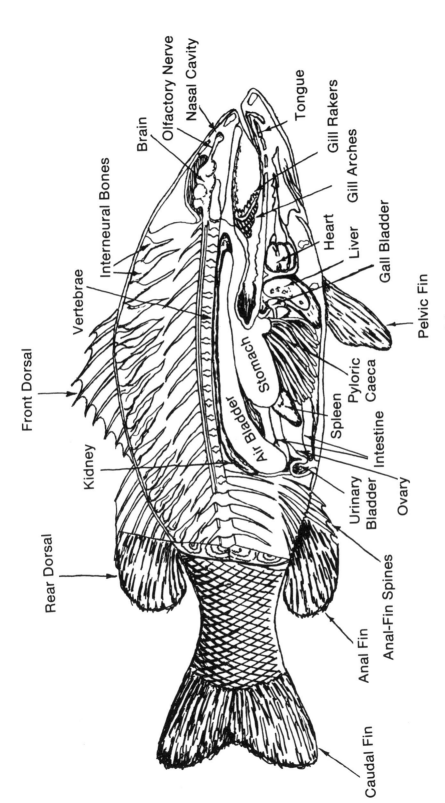

This cutaway view shows the "working parts" of a largemouth bass.

bass. A bass not in good shape will often be stricken in a week.

The fact that Florida-strain bass have survived 39°F. water well is good reason to explore carefully their suitability elsewhere.

Bass Biology Vital to Fishing

The practice of matching your lures to the existing forage in a water body is a good one. You should, however, be aware of a frustrating truth that affects this seemingly logical and simple approach. The presence of a particularly favorite forage species does not guarantee that it will be the type most heavily consumed by bass. In other words, even though the same variety of forage is available in several different water bodies, you can't assume that the bass will feed predominantly on the same type of forage in each place. Let me give you some examples.

Bass love shiner minnows. They'll eat them whenever they get the opportunity. There was a small lake that I regularly used to fish. Later I began diving in it. Early in the season, I was successful with a wide variety of lures. This was during the pre-spawn period. Later, when the heat of late spring had settled into the valley and I waded the shallows, I often spooked schools of small baitfish. They would scurry through the flats like strewn grains of rice and disappear into thick mats of vegetation. Early in the game, I thought these circumstances indicated prime water for minnow-imitating plugs. All signs seemed to point to it. The plugs, however, got less than explosive results in this small pond.

Some years later, when I began to dive extensively in this water, I discovered why. For some reason this lake was the headquarters of some of the largest and latest-blooming polliwogs I've ever seen. On the outside edges of the vegetation mats, the 'wogs would emerge from somewhere in the spongelike maze of decaying bottom debris, wiggle enticingly to the surface until they broke the slick with their blunt noses, then snake downward for the bottom once again.

After a while, I was able to locate the hulking shapes of bass in the shadows at the edge of the thick vegetation. Finally the reason became clear. The largemouths would lurk there to charge out and intercept a polliwog as it descended from its last trip to the surface. It was some of the easiest pickings I've ever seen in the bass world, and the largemouths were taking full advantage of it. The minnows? Well, most of them were on the shallow side of the vegetation mat. I suppose the bass could have bulled their way back to them if they had needed to. They didn't, of course, and that is why we fishermen must beware of our assumptions.

In that lake of the giant polliwogs, I found that dark-hued grubs and cut-off plastic worms worked wonders. They matched the prey that was most easily available to the bass.

The vulnerability of forage is a factor of extreme importance in the bass's lifestyle. The vulnerability or availability of certain forms of prey depends upon several prime factors. These factors include the environment, the weather, and the season of the year. Let's look at each.

The makeup of a river or lake or tidal estuary greatly affects the ease with which a bass can attack different kinds of prey. Had the big polliwogs not been available in the lake I just mentioned, the largemouths would have had to work to get at the shiners that were behind a barrier of weed and algae. The bass could have reached the minnows, but I also noticed that there were bullheads in this small lake. Now if the young of that species were more readily available to the bass—which they might well have been— I'm sure the largemouths would have turned to them. When wind and wave action moved the minnows from the security of the vegetation, I'm sure the bass were standing by to intercept them, just as I've observed in other water bodies.

A lake with timber as the main form of cover provides less security for minnows, and so they're more frequently utilized as part of the bass's diet than they are in some other lakes.

The seasonal vulnerability of prey affects which species the bass utilize most. In some ponds, for example, the polliwogs may have developed into adult frogs earlier in the season. In this case, the bass would take an occasional frog as it became easily available. The largemouths, however, would almost certainly be feeding steadily on some other species. In certain lakes early in the season, and in other lakes slightly later, various forms of salamanders become a regular item in the bass diet. Imitations (or the real thing used as a natural bait) are extremely successful during these periods.

If bass are in prime condition, they're very likely to take a small sunfish of one kind or another. Earlier we discussed the peak periods that adult bass go through during the season. In order to chase and catch a healthy bluegill, for example, an adult largemouth must be in one of these high-cycle stages. Otherwise the little panfish will almost certainly escape.

The thinking angler will be aware of which prey species are available to bass during which periods in the lake he regularly fishes. And to be most successful, he will also keep in mind the existing cover and which bait may be most vulnerable at the time he is fishing. It is important to pay attention to the slightest change in conditions that could affect the feeding of bass, changing them (even for only a short time) from one forage species to another. For example, be aware of the duration of a strong wind that's driving certain prey from cover, or a rainfall that is washing another form of forage into the water.

All of these possible variables may seem to make the choice of lure or bait an impossibly difficult decision. Yet something is definitely in a bass angler's favor. The vulnerability factor works two ways. True, it dictates which prey the bass will be most heavily feeding upon. It also results in largemouths taking advantage of a yet *more* vulnerable species—especially if it is a favorite—if that species suddenly becomes available.

If, for example, the bass have been feeding on salamanders and you suddenly present them with a natural shiner that is obviously injured and is wobbling around helplessly, they are not likely to refuse the offering if they are in any kind of receptive attitude. A similar thing happens when a well-presented spoon or spinner that imitates a wounded baitfish is taken, even though the bass have been feeding on, say, crayfish. In these situations, the key is the presentation. You must make your imitation—or for that matter natural bait—more desirable by making it more vulnerable or more available. Don't present your offering so that a bass must move a great distance to intercept it. Remember the physical characteristics of the largemouth: he is built for short bursts of great speed, not for long-range pursuit.

A largemouth seems to know this limitation—even as it applies to the survival of his offspring. Though guardian bass will pursue natural predators of their eggs and fry, they usually do not chase such predators any great distance. There are exceptions, of course. I have seen male bass chase sunfish in a fairly long-range dodging course that took them away from their nest for far too long a time. During the male's absence, not only bluegills but also other predators—salamanders, little gray eels, turtles—were able to devour greedily many of the bass's eggs.

The bluegill is still the worst predator because these sunfish work together to decimate bass nests. In waters with high bluegill populations, I have observed that nine out of every ten bass nests can be destroyed within the first twenty-four hours by these panfish. In studies by Hugh Barwick of the U.S. Fish and Wildlife Service and Dennis Holcomb of the Florida Game and Fresh Water Fish Commission, in waters that have extremely dense bluegill populations the bass will not even spawn. I have watched the bluegills at work many times while I've been lying on the bottom or observing from some distance in a boat. They are like a pack of tireless hyenas. They wait, hovering around the nest like the spokes of a wheel with the guardian male bass at the hub. If the nest is exposed on three sides, it is a near certainty that it will not survive. With one, preferably two flanks protected, the nest has better survival odds. The bluegills will not just wait patiently. Periodically one will become bold and try to steal eggs while the bass is on the nest. Some observers believe that this bluegill is somehow chosen by his comrades to act as a decoy, but to me it seems more likely that he simply can't restrain himself from going for the choice morsels. His approach is nearly always the same.

If a bluegill is going to take a try at scooping up a few eggs, he is not so stupid as to dive head first into the face of the male largemouth. He will mount his attack from a flank or the rear. The bluegill will nose down and slowly sink toward the nest in this attitude. As soon as the bass notices the bluegill in this position, he will charge out at the intruder.

Guardian bass never try to kill or destroy and devour predators, even the bluegill. The bass, in fact, aren't eating while on nest duty. It's enough that they chase the predator away. In the madcap darting pursuit, the bass may get close enough to nip the offending bluegill. Often he does nothing but drive away the intruder sunfish, which will drift back after a while. While the bass is away, the other panfish that have been waiting in the wings dart in and gulp eggs at a mad rate. When the bass returns, he scatters the feasting bluegills with a quick swirl and series of feints. Then he resumes guard over a somewhat depleted nest.

If the male bass leaves his nest too often, the eggs will all be destroyed. But he can't seem to help himself when a bluegill assumes that head-down posture and slowly descends toward the bottom and his nest.

Duplicating this movement has been responsible for some torrid bass fishing. Glen Lau, after seeing the reaction of bass to this movement by bluegills, designed a lure (previously mentioned on page 136 that would simulate the reaction. At first he tried simply weighting the line in front of the plug. That approach didn't quite result in the right action. Glen experimented with weights on most of the commercially available lures, which either remained suspended when the retrieve was stopped or else began to sink tail first. Nothing seemed satisfactory. Finally Lau had his own plug built with string lead implanted into the lures. The balance was critical. When the retrieve was stopped, the plug had to tip nose down, very slowly, then slowly sink at that angle. After much testing, the proper balance was achieved.

The plug sank at the rate of one foot every 15 seconds. To see how effective the lure would be if presented on target, Lau directed his experimenting fishermen to cast to bass he located underwater. One day, every bass to which the anglers cast took the plug.

This plug's action can trigger the strike response before (and even after) the spawn. Evidently there is still enough latent nest-protective attitude to enrage adult bass that see this bluegill-like movement. In summer, however, a plug with this action is not nearly so effective.

Another biological quirk that's important to remember if you want to increase your fishing success is what might be called the pecking order among bass. In Chapter 1, this factor was mentioned as it relates to holding stations. By now it should be evident that a pecking order—that situation where certain bass take the dominant position or role over others—can affect which largemouths you are fishing over or around, and which may be inclined to take a lure or bait.

I described how the largest bass in supercover inevitably had claim to the densest, most desirable section of that cover. I also related how, when one of the big fish moved away, the spot would be filled by another bass of about the same size until the original fish returned to claim its rights once again.

Don McCoy reported on this phenomenon of large vs. smaller bass in holding areas: "I am now convinced," said McCoy, "that small bass have very different behavior patterns relative to the larger bass. In the first place, the smaller fish are always on the periphery of the preferred holding structure areas. They are also more frequently observed in a free-swimming state. In all likelihood, this is due to the . . . notion of territoriality. . . . Larger fish consistently held the more preferred spots."

Dr. McCoy also mentions how, though larger fish are regularly at the top of the pecking order, smaller fish have no fear of driving the lunkers away during the spawn. "It was frequently observed that a small male bass would attack and drive off a larger fish in order to protect the young fry."

It should be obvious that as fishermen, we are faced with two real problems: (1) the small bass are most frequently in position to get at lures or bait before the larger fish do, and (2) although the big largemouths can have what they want, the feisty smaller fish often take the initiative.

A couple of things can help us to take the bigger bass, though.

• First, the earlier-mentioned condition factor comes into play here. During periods of high condition, the larger bass seem to become more aggressive, knocking lures and baits before the smaller, younger fish can get a crack at them. The smaller fish seem to recognize the signs. When the big fish begin to stir restlessly, finning in place, popping their jaws, and raising their dorsal fins in an alert gesture, the lesser bass hold back.

• The second thing that can aid us in pursuit of the large fish is just the knowledge of the kinds of conditions that help to produce lunker-largemouth country: (1) super-heavy cover—especially if deeper water is nearby, (2) an area of high concentration or else of regular passage of prey that can easily be ambushed without the need for a bass to expose itself very long or at all, and (3) freedom from the constant harassment of man. All these things make up ideal conditions to attract the largest, most desirable bigmouth bass.

In our seasonal pursuits of the largemouth, it is worthwhile to remember the need of choosing the proper water type for the time of year. Much has been written on the virtues of small streams and ponds for early-season bass fishing. But don't forget: the smaller water bodies may, indeed, warm up earlier than the larger impoundments. When this happens, the bass are encouraged to begin their reproductive routines earlier than in the larger water bodies. Sudden weather reversals, as discussed in the chapter on weather, frequently push the small-water largemouths from their beds or send them back into deeper water before the nests have even been constructed. In a larger lake or reservoir, the spring fishing may not start quite so early. But once it does start, we are more likely to be in a period of more stable weather.

I normally look for my early-season bass sport in the smaller waters, but I'm no longer surprised when what started out as a real bonanza in springtime fishing stops suddenly and completely. If there is too much of the erratic weather in early spring, the spawn in the smaller lakes will suffer more than the spawn in the larger water bodies. Usually nature finds a way to rebalance things in a couple of years if left to her own devices. A pond that may have been dubbed "fished out" one year can gain the reputation of a bass factory not too many seasons later.

Curious Bass Behavior and Theories to Ponder

In the discussion on night behavior, I reported that bass— because of the positions in which I found them—most likely did some form of sleeping. I also said I wasn't certain whether my light shocked them and put them into a nonmoving catatonic-like state. I finally satisfied myself that largemouth bass do rest—if not literally sleep as we know it. The reason for this statement is that I eventually located the fish in what could only be described as a dormant or sleeping state by day. The fish were far back beneath weed or algae mats, in cuts in the banks, or in weed-choked coves. They had positioned themselves on their bellies, balanced by their rigid pelvic fins. Their gills moved, but very slowly and evenly. I observed bass in such a state for minutes at a time before they would suddenly seem to awaken and perform another interesting act before moving about.

Upon "awakening" or moving from these dozes or naps, the bass would frequently, not always, go through a movement I began to call jaw popping. Their mouths would open slightly, then snap the rest of the way open while their gills flared. They did this several times over.

Upon subsequent investigation, these movements proved to be a gill-clearing function. Biologists call it coughing, which is a fairly accurate description of the movement. During this behavior, the fish clears its gills of bits of debris that have settled in them. The reason the bass seemed to do this every time they "awoke" during my observations was no doubt because particles collected on their gill rakers during their dormant state.

I later learned that other members of the sunfish family engage in this behavior. So do fathead minnows, trout, and salmon.

So intrigued have biologists become with this coughing that they have experimented with the idea of using captive fish as monitors (or watchdogs) over the quality of certain waters in which industrial wastes are dumped. An apparatus that monitored the number of coughs per minute among fish in electrode chambers could be used as the basis for establishing an indicator scale aimed at determining levels of heavy metals in the water.

Back to my belly-resting fish before they began waking up and coughing. I tried several times to arouse interest in these fish by having a partner in a boat cast and retrieve lures while I watched underwater. The bass remained in their positions, not turning toward or away from the lure. I later performed the same tests with natural baits and saw a similar lack of reaction. I have no doubt that bass just are not about to eat during certain times of the day, and probably the same holds true for certain times of night.

A new theory tries to explain the reason, other than safety, that bass seem to like at least some fairly deep water in their vicinity.

This theory maintains that bass need at least some water deeper than 12 feet in order to digest their food properly. In other words, the added pressure at this depth is necessary for their digestive organs to function properly, and this is why many bass retreat to such depths once they have finished significant feeding.

There may be a germ of truth in this theory. Some bass held in aquariums seem unable to assimilate food properly. Bass held for scientific use will sometimes seem to grow quite fat and healthy-looking on the exterior; however, they may not be in as good shape as they appear. The difficulty may simply be caused by lack of exercise in the confined environment of a tank—or just possibly caused by the lack of depth.

Evidence also seems to indicate that in a natural environment, a soft life can affect various fish just as it does humans, and that the fast-growing, deep-bodied, small-headed fish that have gorged on overplentiful prey may not be in anywhere near as good a fighting shape as some of the slightly leaner fish that have been forced to scramble for their food.

Fat fish seem to suffer from heart disease in the form of a type of arteriosclerosis that most likely leads to anginal attacks. From Dunedin, New Zealand, J. Cleminson reported on the lack of stamina and fighting ability of many deep, heavy fish he has caught.

"I have landed a brown trout of eleven pounds . . . in one minute in the Clinton, a large powerful river," said Dr. Cleminson. "On autopsy, this fish was found to have its stomach filled with mashed potato; the fish had been feeding well from the kitchen of Glade House."

Bass seem not to be immune to the effects of overeating or eating the wrong kinds of food. One of Glen Lau's aquarium bass that seemed in good shape died one day for no apparent reason. The fish underwent autopsy. Everything seemed normal except for one thing: the abdominal walls of the fish contained an abnormal amount of fat. It was the pre-spawn period, and the eggs that were developing in this female seemed to have distended the abdomen as far as possible. The eggs were still expanding and it is possible that as they matured they pressed against the fish's organs enough to inhibit proper function. It was plain to see that because of the fat-lined abdominal walls, the eggs had nowhere else to go.

Had the bass accumulated this extra fat from: (1) a rich diet, (2) lack of exercise, or (3) insufficient water depth in which to descend to assimilate the food? In your fishing, it might be interesting to notice which bass give you the best fight over the long haul—those that are lean or slightly heavy-bellied, or those with huge potguts and smaller heads in proportion to their girth.

Stories have arisen from time to time about bass that have holed up in some impossible den. These bass, it is said, are impossible to catch because they've reduced their normal food intake. Some of these tales hold that such bass have even learned to eat vegetation rather than other fish life. This idea is false. Though bass may come up and roll slowly near heavy vegetation, they cannot consume any of it. Bass lack enzymes such as maltase, amylase, lactase, and invertase, which are necessary for the breakdown of carbohydrates after the consumption of vegetation. Some fish species do posses these enzymes and can eat vegetation. Not the bass. He is a flesh eater.

Among trophy-bass hunters, a question that has long been the subject of cracker-barrel jaw sessions is whether or not largemouth bass change their sex as they age. There is one very good reason for the belief that male bass become females with advancing age: None of the truly big fish caught are ever males. Initially, it seems a far-fetched theory—bass changing sex. But some salt-water species are able to do so. Why not largemouth bass?

As long ago as 1939, biologist Marian James reported finding both male and female reproductive tissue in the organs of several largemouth bass. Still, sex reversal in bass has not definitely been proven as this book goes to press.

Many observers believe that the lack of older, larger males is much more simply explained. These biologists think that as a year-class of largemouths ages, the percentage of males decreases just because the males die at an earlier age than the females. Because bass do not stop growing as they age, their longevity determines their ultimate size. So, say the researchers, this is why fishermen catch larger female bass.

As an aside, it is interesting to note that bass seem to live longer in their Northern ranges. Some of the oldest bass on record include a fifteen-year-old from Wisconsin. The oldest recorded Southern bass was from Louisiana. It was eleven years old.

Sexual maturity of bass is related more to growth and size rather than age. Among the fast growers, a male less than 10 inches long can be mature. Mature females are generally at least 10 inches. It is possible for a bass to mature in its first year of life and be able to spawn by the second year.

The largemouth has an advanced muscle system. The body muscles of bass are made of up red and white tissue. The red-colored muscle is used for sustained swimming, the white for bursts of speed when attacking prey or escaping enemies. Largemouths in warm water can attain speeds of about 12 miles per hour—roughly five times as fast as you can crank a lure.

There has been a lot of discussion about the canniness of largemouth bass, and fishermen who hold to the belief that these fish are the smartest that swim aren't going to like the following:

In tests by experimenter Arthur Witt Jr., bass could not learn to avoid a hook as well as bluegills could. Later experiments by Dennis Radabaugh (on the relative learning ability of largemouth bass and bluegills) showed that the performance of the panfish was far superior to that of the bass.

Maybe this information just means that bass have more resistance to being trained—something like a cat compared to a dog. Who is to say which is "smarter," the cat who stubbornly insists on carrying out its affairs in its own way, or the dog that bows to the supremacy of its master's commands?

Possibly the nature of the cited experiments favored the bluegill. In any event, some people would consider it a disgrace if the lowly bluegill proved to be mentally more highly developed than the bass.

It does seem that male and female bass have about equal learning abilities. But the interesting thing is individuality of bass in the area. Some largemouths just never learn. This is the type of bass that can never resist striking a lure or bait. If you release him, you can always count on some fishing action again in his territory—

even on the slow days. Unfortunately, these fish usually are removed quickly from a water body.

Earlier in this chapter we looked at the ferocity of the male bass while he is guarding the nest and saw how he quickly disperses all predators. There are, however, a couple of interesting exceptions.

The first is a predator: common slow-moving snails. Snails are able to approach and enter the nest without the bass normally becoming overexcited. Snails do consume some eggs, but not as many as other enemies.

The second type of creature allowed to enter a largemouth-bass nest does not seem to be a predator. Researchers Marjorie Carr, Robert Kramer, and Lloyd Smith reported that the male largemouth permits golden shiners and lake chubsuckers not only to enter the nest but also to lay their own eggs in it.

Even more unusual, the male largemouth then aerates and protects the eggs of these species right along with his own, according to the observers. Why should this be so? Is it the same principal at work that we see among birds—some species laying eggs in the nest of another species, eggs whose hatching young enjoy the parental care of the host? Or is it that—in some way we do not understand—the bass knows that he is, in fact, perpetuating food for his youngsters-to-be?

Yet another subject causes much discussion. It involves the eye position of many largemouths that have been caught on hook and line and taken from the water. Not always, but often, the eyes of the bass are tilted down. Anglers describe the eyes as being "locked down." It takes sometimes half an hour for the eyes to return to a normal position on bass that are kept in livewells or on stringers.

The simplest explanation seems to be that the fish was shocked when he was lifted from the water. His balance is totally thrown off once he is removed from an aquatic environment. Some experimenters are beginning to believe that the membranes around the eyes could be a sort of sensing system like sonar, and that the bass use this system for orienting themselves in dingy water, as they use their lateral line. No real work has been done in this area, but one thing is sure: A bass cannot have his eyes in this downward position when striking prey he has located visually. For this the eyes must tilt forward.

The subject of bass movement was mentioned during the discussion in the first chapter on locating bass. Not mentioned at that time was the fact that certain types of prey actually encourage bass to move farther or more often than do other types. Shiners, for example, are not a prey species that encourages distant bass migrations. Shad are. In fact, there is even a difference between the bass movement encouraged by the two main types of forage shad. It appears that there is more bass movement in relation to thread-fin shad than there is in relation to gizzard shad.

Biologist Michael Lembeck is one researcher who has used telemetry for studying bass movements. This is the method that involves the implanting of a small transmitter into the abdominal cavity of bass. Lembeck's work correlated with that of some other observers who used the same techniques. One interesting facet of his studies was that he worked in both clear and naturally dingy waters, to compare bass in distinctly varied environments.

Lembeck learned that the bass in his low-visibility lake seemed to do more moving about than those in the clearer water body. This greater movement was probably because of the natural "cover" the low visibility itself offered. In the clearer water, the bass—before migrating—might remain on one area for a few days or a month. Inevitably they would return to their original locations. Suspended offshore fish were also more frequently encountered in the murkier waters.

Lembeck's "transmittered" bass seemed to confirm what I had learned through underwater research. Some bass migrate near shore; others move offshore. Usually those bass that travel the greatest distances are the fish that swim farthest from the shoreline. Lembeck also learned that after spawning recuperation it was the female bass that traveled farthest. These fish moved on the average of half a mile a day. A move of two to three miles was tops. Some of the monitored females would eventually swim the entire length of the lake.

The male fish, after their nest-guarding duties were completed, remained localized for some time. It was not until the beginning of

July (in the San Diego lakes in which Lembeck did his work) that the male largemouths began to roam.

Much still remains to be learned about the bass's natural day-to-day movements and habits. Still, the information gathered in the past few years on the life cycle of largemouths far exceeds what was known during the past several decades. If we put this knowledge properly to use, it will enable us to enjoy more fruitful sport and perpetuate that sport for future generations of anglers like ourselves. With that in mind, we must next take a look at what our relationship with the largemouth has done to the fish, and at what that relationship will probably do tomorrow.

7

Bass and Man

How to Enter the Bass World

In earlier chapters on vision and sound, we took a look at some of the ways a bass reacts when anglers intrude into his territory. The more involved I became in the bass's world, the more I became aware of factors that may affect your fishing success. These factors, too, relate to invasion into the bass's domain.

I should tell you of the times I spent resting on the bottom in clear water, sometimes kneeling, sometimes leaning back on the bottom of my air tank, breathing as quietly as possible. A lot of that time was spent trying to get a bass-eye perspective of the underwater world around me. Of course that was not completely possible—even physically.

The placement of my eyes in the front of my head, for example, is all wrong for a bass. A fish's eyes are placed on either side of his head. This positioning has much to do with a bass's perspective of things. Eventually I examined some of the research that had been done on fish eyes. It helped clear up a lot of things. Times, for instance, when in shallow water I had easily been able to sneak up behind bass by poling a wide-beam canoe. The bass would let me approach quite close; the lower I crouched, the closer I could move. The research I studied told me that a bass has an area directly behind him that is blind, simply because of the location and mobility of his eyes. That small area, however, is the only one where he cannot see.

A bass is able to see directly ahead and above. It is in these directions, in an arc of about 45 degrees, that he has depth perception. But his vision is not nearly so sharp as it might be in these directions, because he is using the edge of his eyes' retinas with which to focus. A bass can also see to both sides. Objects viewed at right angles to either side of his head are seen sharply. Obviously, this must have been why the bass I observed that were not alarmed would turn sideways in order to examine at leisure some object in which they were interested, including me. You ought to be aware that the bass and other fish also have the ability to see sharply two different things that are happening simultaneously on each side of their head. In other words, there is very little that can go on close around them—especially in fairly clear water—that they cannot see.

One thing I became aware of during those observation sessions on the bottoms of lakes was the condition of the water surface. It is no earth-shattering discovery for me to report that bass must be very much more aware of things entering their world when the surface is dead calm than they are when wind stirs the water surface into a chop. But I began noticing other things as well. During calm days in extreme shallows, I could really see two environments on the surface, depending on how I was situated and on what I concentrated.

When viewing a glass-calm surface, I not only was able to see some overhead objects in the air environment but could also view things on the bottom, reflected by the underside of that calm surface. It is logical that a bass sees about the same thing. I do not know if he can use reflected visions to pinpoint, for example, forage that is moving outside of his direct vision. If he can, then he is no doubt aware of an easy meal on the far side of some cover that blocks his direct line of sight. Maybe this possibility explains why we sometimes catch fish in calm weather while dragging a lure in an area where no fish should logically be.

Another thing I became aware of was the way fishing line breaks the surface in calm weather. Even monofilament is quite obvious as it sits in the surface film. Once it's underwater, it becomes much more difficult to locate, with the exception of certain bright-pigment lines (see Chapter 3 on how bass see).

From underwater, I watched the approach of fishing boats, and in fairly calm water even watched the fishermen themselves. I noticed that when I was able to see anglers in a boat from my location on the bottom, I was more aware of bright-colored clothing than I was of clothing of gray, tan, green, or blue. Yet I can't honestly say that I believe bass become uneasy or spooked by anglers who wear bright clothing. As mentioned earlier, the whole idea of fishing quite near bass cover is to make your approach in a way that does not allow largemouths to become aware of you in the first place. The first thing the fish should notice is your carefully presented lure or natural bait.

In this sequence, a plug-hooked bass is brought to boat.

Here the same fish is released. The visibility of parts of boat and fishermen is very evident.

As I learned when approaching bass from behind in a boat, the fish cannot really see distant objects on the surface if those objects are held at a low angle relative to the surface. In other words, if you remain low in a boat, or cast from a greater distance while standing, a bass will be far less likely to see you. What can happen when you're working somewhat nearer to a fish, however, is that shadows from your rod, fly line, or cast lure may spook the bass. The rod itself may come into a bass's range of vision though you, the angler, do not. I am thoroughly convinced that I have spooked bass holding in the shallows because of these things.

I do not know what kind of threat a rod sticking into a bass's range of vision represents to the fish, but I do know it disturbs largemouths. Perhaps it is the suddenness of the back-and-forth movement of the cast. Yet even a long nonmoving rod slowly extended over a bass's holding position seems to alert the fish at times—not always. Shadows flickering over a largemouth's hole will be more than likely to bring back the learned fear of the fish's youth, wnen any aquatic bird or mammal could descend upon and try to devour him.

What all this boils down to is the need for increased awareness on your part when positioning your boat or self for bass fishing. You must consider the following:

• The angle of sun.
• Water depth (a bass in shallow water will be able to see you more easily than one deeper).
• How much commotion you will make trying to reach a certain spot vs. water disturbance you may make casting from a greater distance.
• Water clarity.
• Calmness of the surface.

Another suggestion for approach has to do with fertile ponds or vegetation-rich bays where a boat is not available. Earlier I mentioned float tubes as a practical and inexpensive means for maneuvering in some bass waters. For certain situations I suggested the use of rubber swim fins—the type used by sport divers—instead of plastic foot flippers. In some really vegetation-thick places you might be better off with no foot equipment whatsoever.

In such situations, I've found it better to work the outside edges of thick vegetation mats with my float tube, just kicking my way along against the plants themselves. Foot fins become too tangled. Usually under these conditions I wear loosely the shoulder harness of my fishing tube. Sometimes I'll come to areas where I can actually walk on a semisoft bottom. Such a bottom will inevitably give way into muck, and at those moments, with the tube worn low and loosely, I'm able to fall forward, elbows on the float, and kick my legs back to avoid getting them stuck in the gumbo. Such swamp-dogging often gets you to places that have not been fished in a very long time.

A float tube rigged as suggested in text is often the ticket to reaching rarely fished backwaters, as Jerry Gibbs is doing here.

Many fishermen who work the backcountry in tubes prefer to include in their tackle a small .22 caliber revolver loaded with varmint shot, in case they are in the territory of water moccasins or big snapping turtles. This is not a bad idea if it's legal in your part of the country.

How Angling Affects Bass

It seems like a very long time ago that we began to emerge from the dark ages of bass fishing. It has been only a few years. In the late 1960s and early 1970s, the largemouth was generally considered—along with a lot of other resources—renewable and undiminishable. When a man went bass fishing it was a mark of pride, a badge of honor to tote home a stringerful of bigmouths. Tournament bass fishing and subsequent increased interest in the species finally triggered the realization that fishing can indeed deplete bass populations. Fishermen reacted.

Early in the development of national tournament fishing, anglers were encouraged to bring their fish back alive. Points were deducted for dead or dying fish. (But usually there were no such regulations in most small local tournaments.) Antifungus chemicals were added to water in which captive tournament bass were held alive for later release. Many studies were done to establish just what percentage of these fish recovered after release. It became evident that the cooler the water and the more gently the bass were handled, the better their chances of pulling through. What also became evident was that largemouths that were caught had an even better chance of survival if they were never put in livewells in boats but were released immediately on the spot.

Some tournaments are now organized around this concept of catch and immediate release, and that is a good thing. For recreational fishing, there's no excuse for us to do anything other than immediately release those fish that we're not keeping to eat. It makes no sense for us to ride around all day with a livewell crammed with fish merely to show them off at dockside at the end of the day.

It is very unlikely that most recreational fishermen will go to the trouble of treating their wells and hands with an antifungus agent. The result: some of the bass released at day's end will perish. It is difficult to understand why many anglers persist in cramming their livewells when the only thing they accomplish besides a dubious ego trip is to hurt their own sport.

I don't mean to say that all fishermen should release all bass on all occasions. What we need is to establish guidelines concerning which fish should be released most of the time and which can stand a moderate harvest. Length limits have been an attempt to manage bass in various waters. They have generally been rather ineffective, mainly because they protected fish of the wrong size.

The seemingly most effective plan for managing largemouth bass seems at first to go against both sound logic and human nature. It maintains that the *largest* bass ought to be the ones released.

Most of the fishermen you know consider those large fish as their personal prizes for skillful angling. And that is just the point. Everyone wants to catch big bass. If the larger fish are returned to the water, they will be able to give pleasure to anglers over and over again.

Right here it is best to dispel the myth that these big fish will not be caught more than once. I personally know of several instances in which huge fish were caught and released over a dozen times. One of the more fascinating challenges in the sport is returning to some spot where you or another fisherman has taken a lunker in the past, with the knowledge that you have an excellent chance to coax him into striking again. When you do catch him again, it is an extremely rewarding experience.

The management plan that stresses the release of large bass is really aimed at improving the quality of the sport. Richard Anderson, leader of the Missouri Cooperative Fishery Research Unit under the U.S. Fish and Wildlife Service, is one of the pioneers in this area of bass management. Through experiments begun in 1965 on a private impoundment, Dr. Anderson readjusted the bass population under the following premise: The best fishing is quality fishing, and quality fishing means catching bass larger than 12 inches.

Anderson imposed the following regulation: Bass between 12

and 15 inches long were to be protected. Smaller fish could be taken.

Here's the reasoning behind the regulation: Under favorable conditions, a bass can grow 8 to 12 inches in one season. You can take about 7 percent of the population of small fish and still have an adequate number coming over into the protected 12-to-15-inch class the next year. Anglers will rarely keep the 8-to-9-inch fish but will often keep the 10-inchers, which are good eating size. Once a bass reaches 12 inches, it begins putting on weight rapidly. These larger fish are the ones that produce more eggs. They are strongest in protecting their offspring; also they provide the finest sport—especially if they're released to be caught many times. The non-protected fish in the year class above 15 inches are far fewer in number throughout most of the largemouth's range. They are not considered to represent the prime breeding stock in the majority of the nation's lakes.

The old concept of a 12-inch minimum limit (to let all bass spawn at least once) is not a critical consideration in maintaining the population. It is certainly not critical if you are trying to maintain the quality of the fishing—the larger bass.

In the smaller impoundments where you have a 12-inch limit and where reproductive success is good, the younger bass begin to stockpile if all are protected. As they become crowded, these young bass consume much of the available food quickly. When this happens, the bass cannot grow at a normal rate. Runt bass cannot consume the larger forage species. So the forage species grow bigger, overbreed, and in turn become stunted as their own food becomes less plentiful.

Had the larger bass been released, they would have consumed the larger forage fish. If some young fish are harvested, as they should be, the remaining young of the year will have enough forage on which to grow quickly.

In test lakes where Dr. Anderson applied his regulations to protect the 12-to-15-inch bass, over 65 percent of the adult bass population was larger than 12 inches. In similar lakes with a 12-inch-minimum limit, the population of larger fish (12 inches and up) was only about 5 percent.

As this book goes to press, several large impoundments in

Missouri are experimenting with a 15-inch-minimum limit, and state fishing lakes in Kansas as well as some additional Missouri community lakes are operating under Anderson's program for quality bass management. The program is also under consideration for some thirty-odd ponds in a multistate cooperative in the Midwest.

Many fishermen and some biologists believe the Anderson plan is excellent as far as it goes. But they would add an additional regulation about true trophy-size largemouths. These fish are caught rarely in most parts of the country except where the Florida subspecies of bass exists. The fishermen and biologists just cited believe that bass *over* 15 inches (or, where they exist, bass weighing 8 to 9 pounds and up) should be taken if an angler so chooses. There are many reasons for this thinking.

Some fisheries experts in the state of Florida reason that the giant bass (those over 8 pounds) have passed the peak years of spawning. Since the true lunkers are invariably females, the feeling is that this class of giants occupies too many male bass, keeping them from more-fertile smaller females. Other critics say that the monster-size bass eat more than their share of available forage, plus too many younger bass.

More studies need to be done in this area, but one thing is clear: If more trophy-size bass are kept, then fewer will be available to give repeated pleasure to anglers. Many professional guides in the range of Florida-strain bass—which, because of stocking, now extends across the Southwest and into California—are now imposing a rule upon their clients: no giant bass is kept unless the fisherman wants it for mounting or the fish breaks the angler's personal size record for bass. As pressure increases on trophy bass, such regulations make sense.

Across the country, many anglers are experimenting with Dr. Anderson's bass-management techniques on small private ponds and lakes. Tony Ciuffa of Creve Coeur, Missouri, is one. Tony has been lucky enough to have access to lakes where fish-for-sport is the rule in force. In such situations, when not even the smaller bass are regularly harvested, as they are in Dr. Anderson's methods, Tony has found that attempts at total stockpiling of bass are no good either. What Ciuffa feels would work, however, is remote catch-

and-release zones on our big impoundments. Anglers could fish those zones for sport. Such areas could, if habitat permitted, also act as rearing grounds to replenish areas in the same big lake where catch-and-keep bass fishing is permitted.

In his fishing experiments, Ciuffa also confirmed the reason that schooling bass tend to slacken their aggressive feeding behavior as the season wears on. Ciuffa and a partner worked hard on a school of bass just to see how many fish they could catch. Two of them took and released sixty fish in one day. The two anglers quickly learned that if they hoped to maintain such success with the schooling bass, each fish had to be released on the spot.

As more of the bass in a school that is utilizing deep structure are removed, the school first loses its aggressiveness and then tends to break up. Ciuffa tried moving fish that he had caught from two separate schools into another area that contained the same seemingly ideal deep-water holding structure but was several miles from the capture sites. (Ciuffa and his partner had taken roughly a combined number of thirty fish from two separate schools, planting them in the new area.) These fish were never again encountered at the release site.

What really upset the experimenting anglers was that one of the schools from which the transplants had been taken stopped feeding actively as a school unit immediately after their ranks had been thinned, and did not resume active feeding for the rest of the season. The second school continued to produce striking fish, but far fewer than it had before. By contrast, several other schools on the lake remained just as active as before, until cold weather eventually slowed them up. Ciuffa also reaffirmed that if bass populations in a lake are reduced drastically, schools are far fewer.

It is not only the schooling bass that provide the opportunity to catch good numbers of fish in a single outing. During warm weather, adult bass seem to go through cycles of activity. Every six days or so, the mature fish feed voraciously for four or five hours. During such periods, they can swim down a bluegill on the run, a feat that normally is extremely difficult for them unless they have ambushed the sunfish.

Such periods of frantic activity happen less often in colder weather. But when they do, it is very easy to take a lot of fish. Some anglers do so, though they are only hurting their future fishing.

Releasing Fish

All right. Maybe you're convinced that releasing fish isn't such a bad idea. But isn't a bass damaged during the catch process beyond the point where he can usually recover? Sometimes, definitely yes. With a little knowledge, though, you can easily release nearly all your fish in good shape. A fish caught on a single hook is normally easier to de-barb than one that has taken a treble hook or two. As almost everyone knows these days, it's best to handle a bass as little as possible before releasing him. Sometimes it's possible to perform the release operation right in the water by simply holding the lure or hooks and shaking. This is most often true with a single hook.

Another precaution that is being taken by anglers who care about their sport is dipping the hand that jaw-holds the fish into an antifungicide, or even noniodized salt, before touching the fish. Nets are bad to use unless they're of the rubber-mesh type. A net not only usually prolongs the release process but also is likely to break the protective mucus barrier that covers the fish's body.

A bass that is gut-hooked can be released, and he will usually live if the hook can be properly removed. If a deeply swallowed hook is not removed, the bass's chance for recovery is less.

To remove a deeply swallowed hook from a bass, it's best if two men work together. You'll need long-nosed pliers. It is sometimes possible to grasp the hook with pliers, then back the hook down (down the gullet farther) using a little force. Once the barb is free, turn the hook and carefully withdraw it.

If this approach does not work, you'll have to pull the point toward you through the tissue until the point is exposed. Then you pinch the barb down and back the hook down as just explained. You must reach quite far down the bass's throat to perform this operation. But once you've done it a couple of times, it's not difficult.

The main danger to bass and other fish is complete exhaustion. They can survive handling and even some fungus. But if they have been exhausted by being played too long, they're in great danger. According to research done by the Texas Parks and Wildlife Department, such stress breaks down red blood cells, lowering the bass's ability to take and hold oxygen. If an internal bacterial or viral infeciton strikes the bass during the time it takes him to recover from being caught, the infection will probably kill him. The more fatigued the fish, the longer it takes for him to recover fully.

What about largemouths that break away with a bait hook or lure? It depends on where the fish is hooked and how. It's true that nonstainless hooks eventually begin to corrode and rust. Not stainless. But usually before that happens completely the normal body process of the fish will reject a foreign object such as a hook. That's why it's difficult to tag fish successfully for research. The section of fish tissue surrounding the foreign object actually breaks away in time, taking the offending object with it. Then the true healing process begins.

Though many deeply hooked fish die when a hook cannot be removed, quite a few survive. I have seen and caught fish that had hooks working their way through the side of the bass. On some, the hook was only partially through. On others, the hook was virtually past and holding on by a thread of tissue. It seemed as though the hook had come all the way through the bass's body from inside.

We hear of the same thing happening to human beings—bone splinters or bits of metal or glass being rejected years after they entered the body. I'm sure similar things happen with most living creatures. The only such situation in which a bass has precious little hope of surviving is one in which—because of some freak twisting—the fish has suffered substantial gill damage.

You can release largemouths. It is more than likely that the fish you put back will be one of the really aggressive individuals. In the very near future, he will almost certainly strike again. Just think what a poor lake, bay, sound, or river you would have if all the aggressive bass—the ones that hit lures—were removed, leaving nothing but the recalcitrants whose feeding is more than likely done at night or deep where a fisherman never reaches.

Years ago, when I returned my first bass to the water, I felt rather odd. Not especially happy. But I thought about that fish far into the night. The next time I released a fish, I remembered him, too. And suddenly it was a very good feeling indeed, one that will continue to be nourished as long as I am able to fish for large-mouths.

Hands-Off Policies No Longer Work

Certain groups of people today maintain that all of nature—her lakes, forests, oceans, and rivers; her creatures of the air, water' and earth—would suddenly flourish if man simply stepped back and said something like "OK, we'll no longer interfere."

That shortsighted approach, of course, would never work unless man took far more than a step back. We'd have to do something like completely vacating the planet. So inexorably involved are we with the more primitive world that the only thing left for us is to use whatever means we have to help rectify the damage we have caused over the centuries.

With water bodies, man alone has not caused the deterioration. The inland waters of the world are, like all living things, undergoing an aging process. This process, if taken far enough, means that a lake utterly disappears, swallowed up in swamp. Depending on the location and size of the water body, the process (eutrophication) takes years or centuries. Man, however, causes the eutrophying process to accelerate in numerous ways. Anything that enriches the water will do it. Over enrichment results in plant and tiny animal life blooming and dying, building up ever-deeper layers of quicksand-like silt. Not only is such a neck-deep bottom of silt bothersome to divers who try to spy on bass but it also suffocates life—including the spawn of the largemouth. It kills vegetation, too, turning good holding cover into barren wastes. If the silt can be controlled, kept to the deeper levels rather than piling up on the hard points and gravel ledges where bass spawn, then we have accomplished something.

Biologists have at least made the eutrophying process more palatable in some of the nation's top bass lakes. The state of

Florida is a prime example, and the classic case is Tohopekaliga.

What happened to Toho, and what is scheduled to happen to other lakes in Florida, is the process known to anglers as drawdown. Basically it is a process that gives these aging lakes a spurt of life for about six years. With the water level kept down for a year or so, lakeside homeowners are high and dry. But so are the banks and reefs and points of the lake. Vegetation grows anew in these areas, trapping an abundance of living things as it grows. When the lake level is once again raised, there is an immediate fish explosion. Spawning success rises sharply; young bass feed on the organisms in the new vegatation. Little fish and big fish grow quickly. For a time, bass fishing is superb.

Unfortunately, drawdown is not a long-term solution. It can be (and often is) repeated when the fishing begins to fall off again. But the operation can be quite involved. Often one of the greatest hurdles is to convince lakeshore landowners to accept a period of muddy dooryards and the stench of rotting vegetable and animal matter. Learning to cope with water hyacinth is also not a long-range answer. Fishermen have learned that they can fish past this waterway-choking plant import. They carry a rake or hoe aboard a boat and literally rake an opening in the hyacinth beds in which to drop a lure or bait. Other anglers send live shiners in under the mats and let them swim there. Still, excessive choking by water plants must be controlled by man if he wants to enjoy the sport of bass fishing.

Fish-and-game departments, because of a lack of manpower and funds, cannot offer long-term solutions to these problems. The people who can help are fishermen.

One group in Tulsa, Oklahoma, discovered just how much bass fishermen can do. The Oklahoma Fisherman's Association was a club devoted to occasional tournaments and a good time. The bass fishing had begun going downhill in the state and one man—one of the original tournament anglers in the nation—thought that something ought to be done about it.

"I got to thinking that I was responsible for starting a lot of the pressure on bass," said Don Butler, "so I went to our fisheries division and asked them what we could do."

The division had just drawn up its lake-management plans,

which included everything that ought to be done in each lake in Oklahoma but—because of little money—never would be done. Butler and the Oklahoma Fisherman's Association reviewed the management plans and decided that they could do some of the work.

The fishermen went to the biologist of each region in which they believed they could help. Initially the fishermen built 50,000 tires' worth of artificial reefs. The worn tires were donated. Next they rounded up every old Christmas tree they could find; during a period of low water the fishermen "planted" them vertically as cover. Now, more important, they have planted willow trees at the high-water lines of various lakes. These will grow and provide the vital littoral-zone cover that bass and minute aquatic life need.

To further improve spawning where silt has occurred from rotting vegetation, the fishermen aim to anchor old tires and fill them with gravel. These will be readily accepted by largemouths as spawning beds. The fishermen are planning a series of nursery ponds that will supply 7-inch bass during years of poor spawning. Such a pond is financially out of reach for a bass fishermen's club. But the first of such holding ponds planned by the group was made possible through donations. Local business people supplied valves, an evacuation system, pipes, concrete, and other necessities. The first pond built by the Association was a ten-acre impoundment that supported 3,000 little bass per acre.

The Oklahoma bass fishermen have taken a cue from Ducks Unlimited. Now they have an annual dinner at which prizes donated by fishing-tackle manufacturers and others are raffled or auctioned. The money thus raised goes to help finance the work of this group. If a national organization under the banner Bass Unlimited rises from such efforts, it might well go far to preserve the largemouth and his habitat.

But local bass clubs, chapters of national and regional bass organizations like B.A.S.S., could do a great deal on their own in much the same way that local Trout Unlimited or private trout clubs work to improve their sport. The projects involve work weekends. Here men, women, and kids can pitch in on projects aimed at improving the bass's lot in life.

Of course all habitat-improvement projects, if not on private ponds, must be approved by your local fisheries biologists, but the possibilities are endless. They can include major work such as that being done by the Oklahoma Fisherman's Association. They can be as simple as thinning out panfish such as bluegills (bream). That's a great way to help turn kids on to fishing. If you as an adult put aside your tackle to help a youngster really fill a stringer of bluegills, you'll take a big step forward in building his or her interest in fishing. Plus it helps bass—especially in small ponds.

Planting willows and other cover is an excellent project, as is clearing passageways in ultra-heavy vegetation. It pays to have members of your club (or you as an individual) watchdogging the various lakes and reservoirs in your area. Find out what authority is responsible for water levels, and who could be fiddling with flows. Holding back water from spawning areas in spring, or flooding when it's not needed, can severely hurt the bass population. Frequently pressure can be brought to bear on the minders of the dams to time their flows in harmony with the lake's living creatures.

You also should keep an eye out for illegal netting and for pollutants that might enter the water. All the destruction caused to local waterways must be initially fought at the local level. The burden of preserving aquatic life really falls first on sportsmen.

Another simple but excellent project is building artificial beds for bass. They could be something like the staked-down old tires filled with gravel that the Oklahoma anglers are working on. You can also build extremely effective artificial nests with plastic washbaskets or wire screening. This idea originated with Glen Lau, who, while filming his documentary *Bigmouth*, observed over many hours just how bluegills go about destroying bass eggs. Lau's conclusion was that a largemouth would be far more successful in protecting his eggs if he had only the area above him and one flank to guard.

Lau did a little experimenting. He hollowed out a hole beneath a bank and lined it with gravel and grasses. During the spawning period, bass readily used the diver-made nest. In fact there were four separate spawns in four months in his nest. The amazing thing is that every one of the spawns was successful.

You don't have to be a diver scooping out nests for fish. As suggested, the plastic washbaskets available nearly everywhere, baskets of wicker (though they will not last as long) or wire screening, formed to the proper circular basket shape, can make excellent protectable nests for largemouths.

How to Build a Bass Nest

To make a nest, first you need to cut an opening of about 10 inches in one side of the 10-inch-high basket. Next, line the basket with brushed burlap. A weight of about two pounds is attached on the basket bottom to hold it solidly down.

The nests should be sized for the bass that will use them. For most largemouths, an 18-inch-diameter bottom is fine. But if you're making nests that will be used by the Florida subspecies of largemouth, a bottom diameter of 21 inches is better. The sides should taper out toward the top. The top should have a diameter of about 24 inches normally, 26 to 27 inches for the larger bass. The sides should be only about 10 inches high, which means most washbaskets will need to be cut down.

Of course these nests should be placed in shallow areas where bass have previously been known to spawn. A bass, with only the open top and one area in front of him to guard, will almost certainly produce a successful spawn from such a nest.

As a bonus, he will be less fatigued when the spawn is over and thus much more likely to survive.

By building nests for bass, you will be assisting the mature largemouths two ways: (1) actually encouraging the survival of larger bass in a lake, and (2) encouraging the survival of their spawn. Naturally you should get permission to place such devices in any nonprivate lake.

Hybrids

As man has done with flowers, vegetables, and some domestic animals, he is attempting to produce superior strains of bass through crossbreeding. It is possible that certain of these bass strains will be very well suited to particular environmental situations—even better suited than original strains. So far, no such bass has appeared.

The crosses between smallmouth and largemouth bass have been well publicized and as this book goes to press are still under way. The result has been an extremely aggressive fish. In a natural situation, largemouths and smallmouths do not crossbreed. But the hybrids do. The hybrids will also breed back with the pure-strain parent species (normal largemouth or smallmouth bass). This factor is what worries scientists. They fear that damage might be done to the genetic lines of normal bass through excessive backcrossing with hybrids.

Also, any new biological program is costly. This one is no exception. If biologists should prove that no threat exists from the hybrids to the parent species, it would not be feasible presently for fisheries managers to introduce the hybrids in great numbers into public fishing waters. The program, however, is fascinating and should lead to additional knowledge about bass. Still, we must ask ourselves: do we ultimately want a man-made creature for our sport, or do we want one that is as wild as the ancient predecessors from which it sprang?

8

Reflections on Bass Watching

Looking back on my comments about the difficulties fishermen have in approaching bass, I remember how it was when I first attempted serious underwater observations of largemouths. The problems seemed far more difficult than any fishing situation I had ever encountered.

In the first place, the noise of exhaling compressed air underwater is particularly offensive to largemouths. It is far easier to move close to a largemouth bass in moderately shallow water if you are easing along on the surface breathing through a snorkel.

By and by, the bass I watched in different places around the country would become accustomed to me in my scuba gear. Still, an especially forceful expellation would send the fish fleeing. Slow, quiet breathing was the ticket. And for really getting close, I found it necessary to hold my breath. I learned that the longer you spent with one group of fish the less fearful they became. But largemouths are, in the final analysis, more difficult to put at ease than smallmouth bass. Smallmouths seem far more curious about a diver and will come much closer to watch him.

During my dives, my belief in the individuality of largemouth bass was strengthened many times. I saw during tests with bait and lures that some bass were usually more aggressive than others. During spawning seasons, the same thing held true both in mate selection and in the protection of nests. Some bass were far more curious about me than were others. The curious ones would either allow me to come closer to them or would circle around and around while I pivoted in place. Other individual fish that I began to recognize (no, not all bass look alike) would never come very near, and a few would always flee when I approached.

How was it possible to recognize which fish were which? It became obvious after working around the same groups for a time. Either there would be some physical difference—a marking pattern, odd proportion, or physical oddity—that would enable me to pick out certain fish, or else certain individuals would keep a particular position for long periods of time, either among a group or alone in one location. Certainly they would move from time to time or with a change of season, and then I would need to spend a while determining if I had indeed located an individual fish again.

I learned while working with other divers that some persons seem to have what we termed fish appeal while others didn't. In other words, the fish would allow some of us to come closer than they would others. I may be banished forevermore by members of a certain movement for saying it, but as the months passed it became obvious that bass were generally somewhat more wary of women divers than they were of men.

I was hesitant at first about making such a judgment. Later I learned that some top divers around the nation have also noticed the phenomenon. It may have something to do with the fact that many women really do not particularly care for fish. Perhaps there is some kind of subtle anxiety that is transferred to the fish—even in the form of more active, thus noisier, breathing underwater.

Now, at the end of a period of long, skin-withering sessions at the bottoms of lakes, reservoirs, springs, and streams—plus days and nights afloat in boats, rafts, and tubes—I have learned one thing perhaps not emphasized enough in the pages you have just read: *Although the behavior and habits of largemouths are to a large degree predictable, there is still a very strong element of unpredictability about the species.*

In some ways, I would like to know it all. Yet a stronger feeling makes me glad there is so much we still don't know about the innermost workings and forces that control the largemouth bass.

For what would the forests be without the tingling sepulchral voice of the great horned owl? Who is it with so little vision that he would devise a computer grid to chart the course of every great blue marlin in the sea?

I hope that what I have learned may increase your appreciation of a creature at once complex and simple. And I trust that in your lifetime there will yet be eagles' aeries and that special part of largemouth-bass fishing still cloaked in mystery.

Index

Algae, 60, 167
Anderson, Richard, 181-183
Angling, 180-185
Arteriosclerosis, 168
Autumn weather conditions, 44-46
"Awakening" behavior, 167

Bait-casting (levelwind) tackle, 146
Bankholes, 19-26
  bait for, 37-38
  tackle (in the North), 39-40
  tactics for fishing, 35-39
  technique for, 36-37, 40
Barwick, Hugh, 163
Bass Anglers Sportsman Society
  (B.A.S.S.), 25, 135, 189
Bass fishing:
  factors affecting success, 175-192
  how they strike lures, 115-147
  light and color considerations, 67-93
  location and behavior, 3-39
  natural history, 149-173
  reflections on, 193-195
  sounds and, 95-114
  weather considerations, 41-65
  See also Largemouth bass
Bass nest, how to build, 191

Bigmouth (documentary film), 190
Biology knowledge (vital to fishing),
  160-166
Boat control, wind factor, 54
Boat noise, 97-104
  electric motor, 99-104
  oars or paddles, 98
Boat positioning, precision in, 35
Breckenridge, Rayo, 141-142
Brown, Leroy, 137

Canter, Dr. Mark, 61, 79
Casting rods, 146-147
Ciuffa, Tony, 183-184
Clear water, 8-10
  color preferences, 83
  lines and line weight, 88-93
  response to plastic worms in, 124
  translucent lures for, 87
Cleminson, J., 168
Clugston, James, 58-59
Clunn, Rick, 135-136
Cold-weather environment, 60-65
  finding the fish, 63-64
  using vertically jigged lures, 64-65
Color considerations, 82-93
  how color reacts, 85-86
  and lures, 86-87

Courting behavior, types of, 152-154
Currents, *see* Wind

Day-to-day behavior, theories about, 166-173
Distress vibrations, 109-110
Ducks Unlimited, 189

Electric motor boat sounds, 99-104
  at high speed, 101
  from inconsistent vibration, 101-104
  at lower rpm's, 100-101
  strong vibrations, 101-102
  while trolling, 101
Environmental conditions, bass strike and, 132
  cold-weather, 60-65
  hot-weather, 55-60
Eye control (monocular vision), 68-70
  light entering, 70
  receptors in, 70-71
  See also Vision and visibility

Feather (or hair) jigs, 125-126
Fishing success, factors in, 175-192
  angling, 180-185
  building a bass nest, 191
  hands-off policies, 187-191
  how to enter the bass world, 175-180
  hybrids, 191-192
  releasing fish, 185-187
Flippin' technique, 26-29, 126
Fluorescent-finish lures, 86-87
Flyrods, 146
Frontal systems, 46-49
  oxygen readings, 48-49

Gibbs, Jerry, 179
Gliebe, Dave, 135
Grasses, 13-14

Hall, Porter, 38-39
Hands-off policies, habitat and, 187-191
Hearing ability, *see* Sounds

Holcomb, Dennis, 163
"Home territory," 42
Hot-weather environment, 55-60
  schooling periods, 57-58
Houston, Jimmy, 25-26
Hybrids, 191-192
Hydrophone (device), 104-106

Individualism, bass strike and, 137-138
  unpredictability, 193-195

James, Marian, 169
Jiggerpoling method, 27

Largemouth   bass   *(Micropterus salmoides)*:
  adaptability of, 149-150
  behavior and theories, 166-173
  biology knowledge (vital to fishing), 160-166
  growth and weight, 157-160
  natural history of, 149-173
  renewability of, 42-43
  spawning factors, 150-157
  See also Bass fishing
Lau, Glen, 74, 133, 142-143, 164, 168, 190-191
Learning abilities, 170-171
Lembeck, Michael, 133-134, 172-173
Light and color, 67-93
  color preferences, 82-93
  how it reacts, 85-86
  lines, 87-93
  lures, 86-87
  moon phases, 81-82
  night fishing, 76-80
  sensory abilities, 75-76
  vision and visibility, 67-75
Lines:
  color and type of, 87-93
  underwater illumination, 90
Location and behavior, 3-39
  bankholes and undercuts, 19-26, 35-39
  clear water, 8-10

roaming activity, 10-11
schooling periods, 11-12
shoreline area, 15-16, 19-21
in supercover, 12-39
   tactics for, 26-39
vegetation, 13-14, 16-18, 29-35
wind and currents, 6-8
Lorio, Wendell, 11
Lures:
cold-weather environment, 64-65
color and, 86-87
fluorescent-finish, 86-87
and odors, 75-76
for striking, 115-117
   environmental conditions, 132
   individualism and, 137-138
   physical condition and, 132-134
   plugs, 127-128
   positive and negative responses, 138-145
   shiner minnows, 130-131
   size and season, 134-137
   soft-plastic, 116-126
   spinnerbaits, 128-130
   tackle, 145-147
sounds and, 104-115
   distress vibrations, 109-110
   feeding behavior, 111-112
translucent, for clear water, 87
See also names of lures

McClanahan, John D., 38-39
McCoy, Donald F., 82-83, 93, 126, 134-135, 144, 165
Mann, Tom, 137-138, 141
Martin, Bobby, 32, 124
Metallic finishes, negative reactions to, 87
Miller, Rudolph, 25
Minnows (Cyprinidae family), 76
Missouri Cooperative Fishery Research Unit, 181
Moon phases, 81-82
Morris, Johnny, 124
Mr. Twister (lure), 24

Muscle system, 170

Negative responses, lures and, 138-145
Night fishing, 76-80
   moon phases, 81-82
   warm weather, 80
Nympho (lure), 20

Odors, 74
   and lures, 75-76
Oklahoma Fisherman's Association, 188

Phillips, Billy, 25
Photosynthetic reversal, 60
Physical condition, bass strike and, 132-134
Plastic lures, *see* Soft-plastic lures
Plastic-tail grubs, 125-126
Plugs, 127-128
Positive responses, lures and, 138-145
Pow-RR jig head, 24

Radabaugh, Dennis, 170
Rahn, Dennis, 152
Releasing fish, 185-187
Retractor lentis muscle, 70
Roaming activity, 10-11

Schooling period, 11-12
   hot weather, 57-58
Seasons:
   bass size and, 134-137
   weather considerations, 43-46
Sensory abilities, 75-76
   during night feedings, 78
   sounds and, 95-114
   vision and visibility, 67-75, 175-176
Sexual maturity, 169-170
Shiner minnows, 130-131, 160
Shoreline, shape and composition of, 15-16; *See also* Undercut shoreline
Short-term weather lore, 46-49
Siler, James, 58-59

Snagless Sally (lure), 20
Snails, 171
Soft-plastic lures, 116-126
Sounds, 95-114
    bass's lateral line (inner ear) and, 95-
        97
    boat noise, 97-104
    lures and, 104-114
Spawn factors, 150-157
    courting behavior, 152-154
    favorable conditions, 150-152
    guarding the nest, 154-156
    number of eggs, 154
    post spawn period, 156-157
Spinnerbaits, 128-130
Stearns, Bob, 111
Storms, 49-53
    activity curtailment, 51
    and downpour, 49-51
    electrical disturbances, 52
    feeding periods, 51, 53
    rains of longer duration, 52-53
Subria weedless jig, 20
Summer weather considerations, 44
    hot-weather environment, 55-60
    storms and downpour, 49-50
Supercover, bass in, 12-39
    bankholes and undercuts, 19-26
    fallen-down tree area, 16-18
    lures and, 20-22, 24
    old bridge supports, 22-23
    and precise boat positioning, 35
    shallow or deep water, 25
    shoreline area, 15-16, 19-21
    tactics for fishing, 26-39
    timber mazes, 14-15
    vegetation and, 13-14, 16-18

Tackle, 145-147
    for undercuts and bankholes (in the
        North), 39-40
Telemetry, 172
Texas Parks and Wildlife Department,
        186
Thomas, Dee, 26, 27, 126
Timber mazes, 14-15

    tactics for fishing, 26-29
Translucent colors, 86
Trees, fallen-down, location areas of,
        16-18

Ugly Bug (lure), 24
Undercut shoreline, 19-26
    baits for, 37-38
    tackle (in the North), 39-40
    tactics for fishing, 35-39
    technique for, 36-37, 40
Underhand flipping cast, 28-29
U.S. Fish and Wildlife Service, 163,
        181

Vegetation, 13-14, 16-18
    fallen-down tree areas, 16-18
    photosynthetic reversal, 60
    tactics for fishing, 29-35
Vibro-Tail jig, 24
Vision and visibility (how bass see), 67-
        75, 175-176
    dim light safety, 71-73
    eye control, 68-70
    eye receptors, 70-71
    light debate, 70
    water correlation, 73
    within 15-foot radius, 74-75

Warden, Robert, Jr., 11
Warm weather, night fishing, 80
Weather considerations, 41-65
    cold environment, 60-65
    feeding periods, 41-42
    hot environment, 55-60
    kinds of, 41
    seasons, 43-46
    storms, 49-53
    trends (frontal systems), 46-49
    and water correlation, 73
    wind, 53-55
Wig-Wag Minnow (lure), 24
Wind, 53-55
    and currents, 6-8
Witt, Arthur, Jr., 170
Wright & McGill Model 84 hook, 38